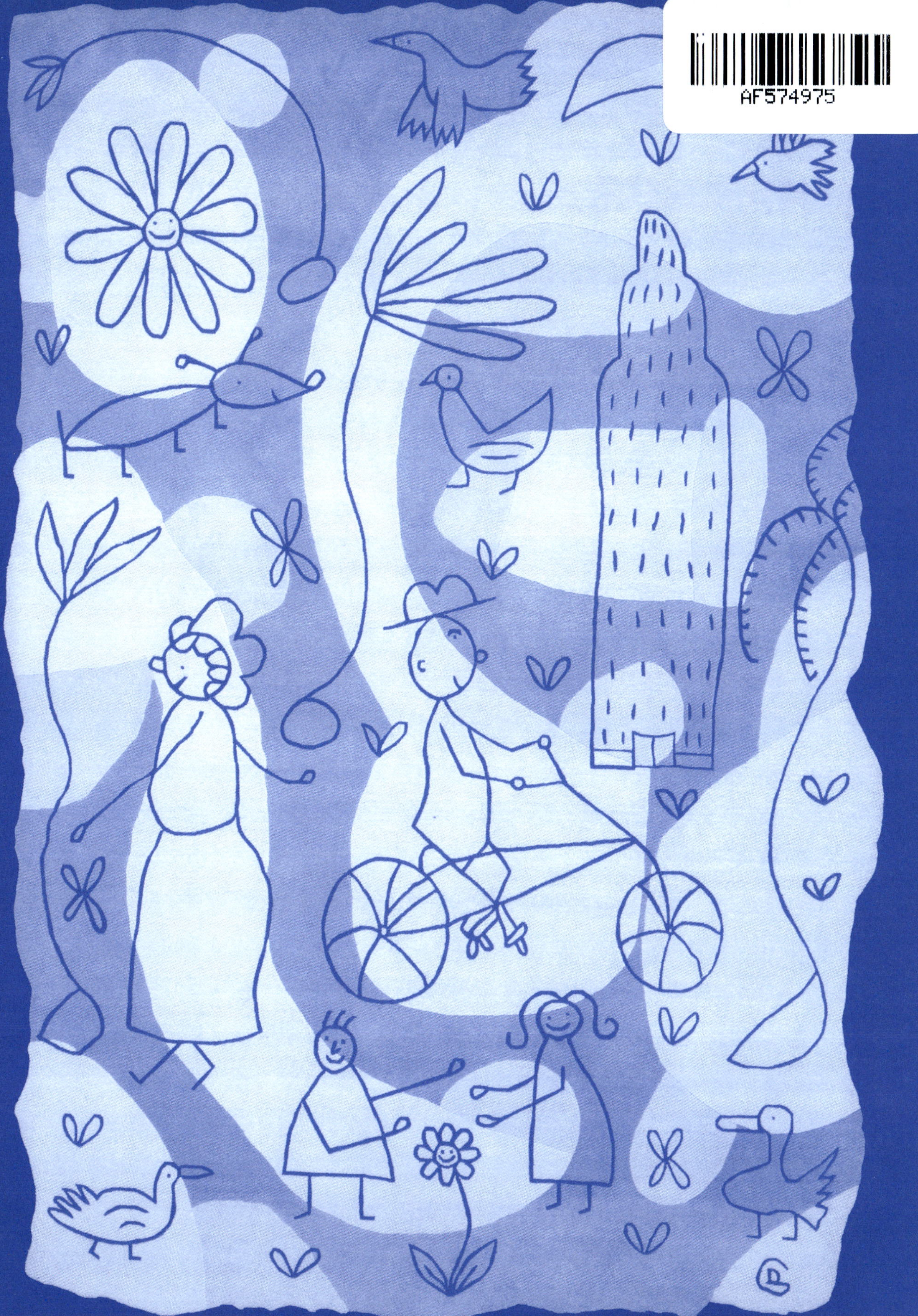

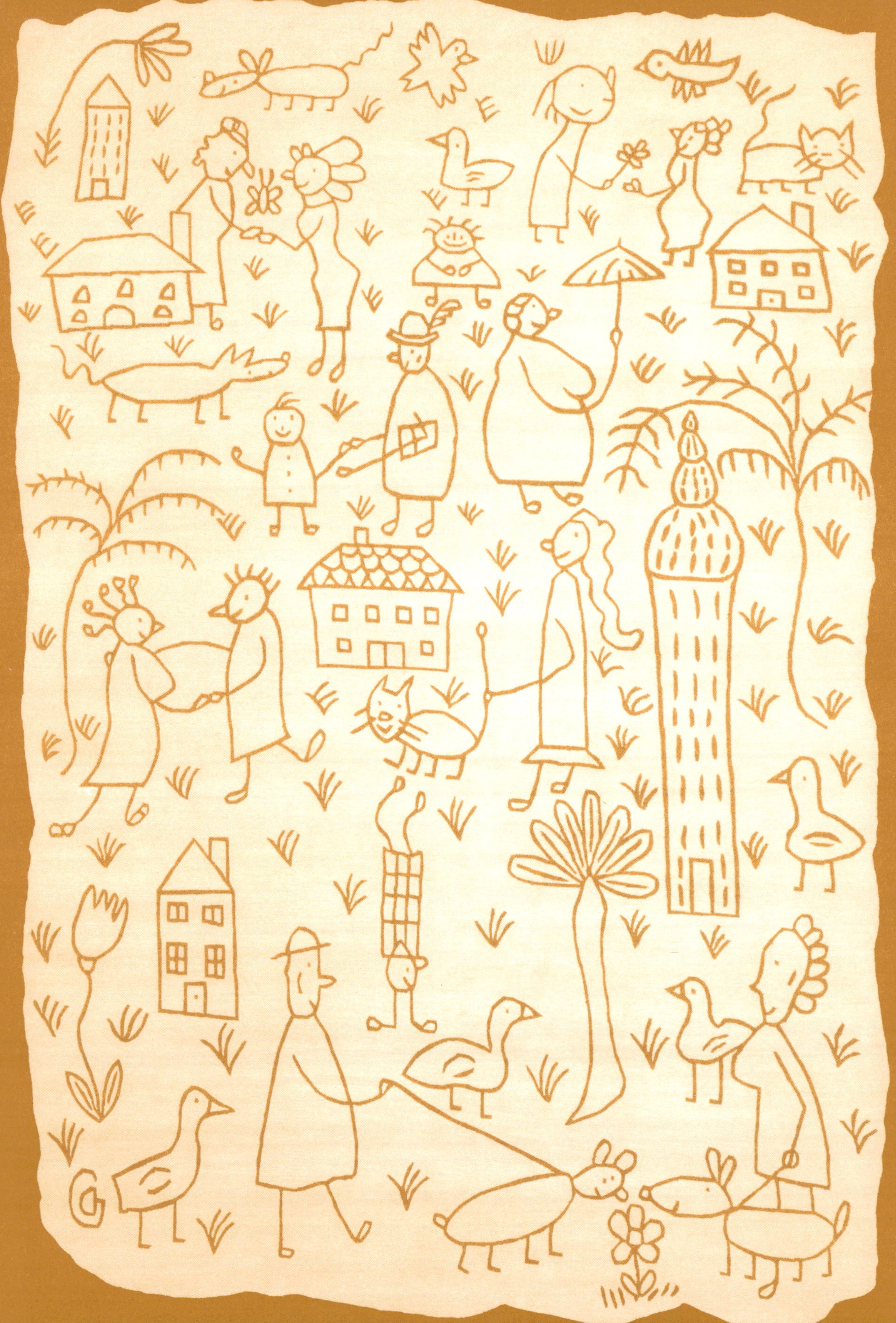

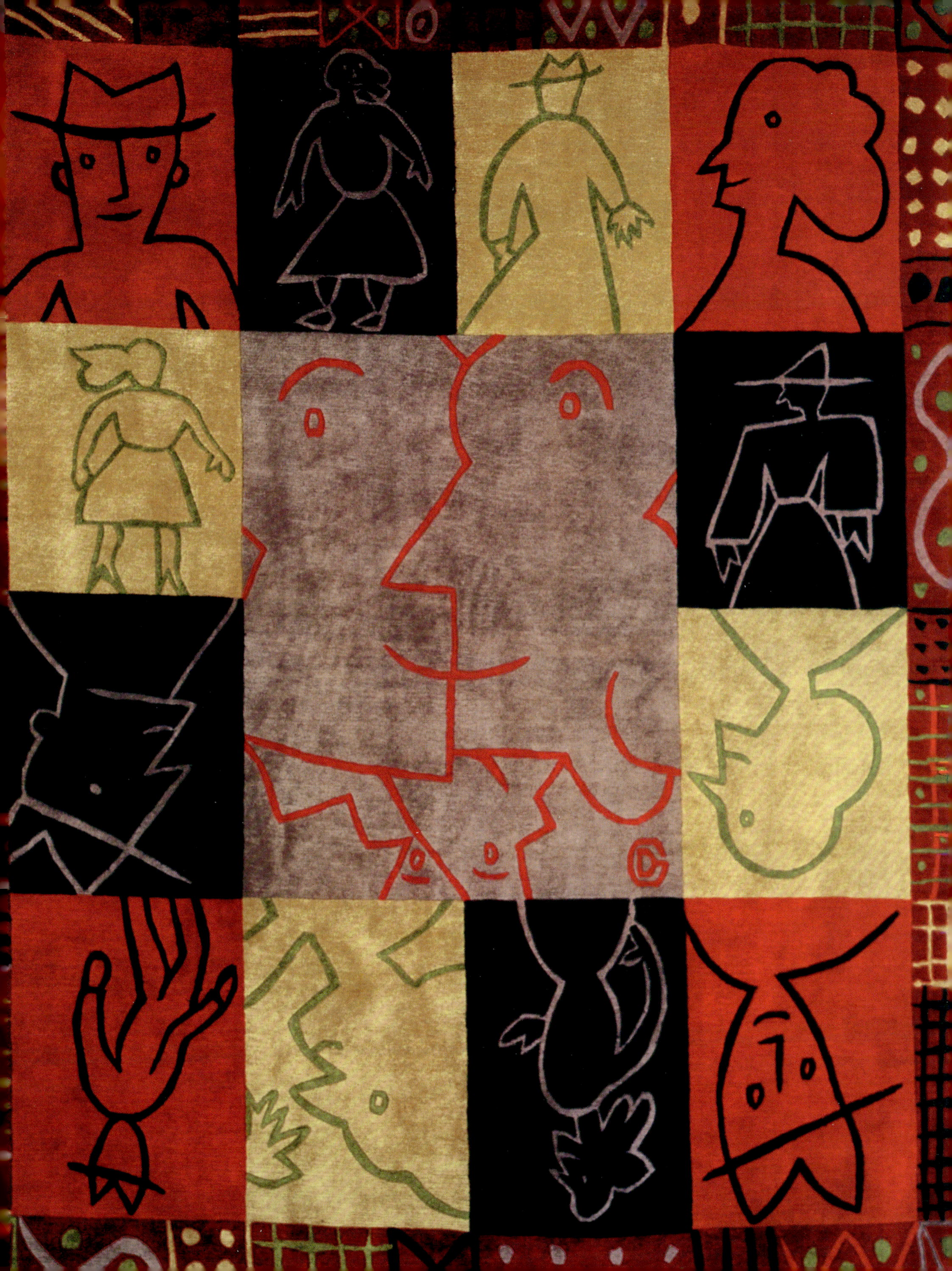

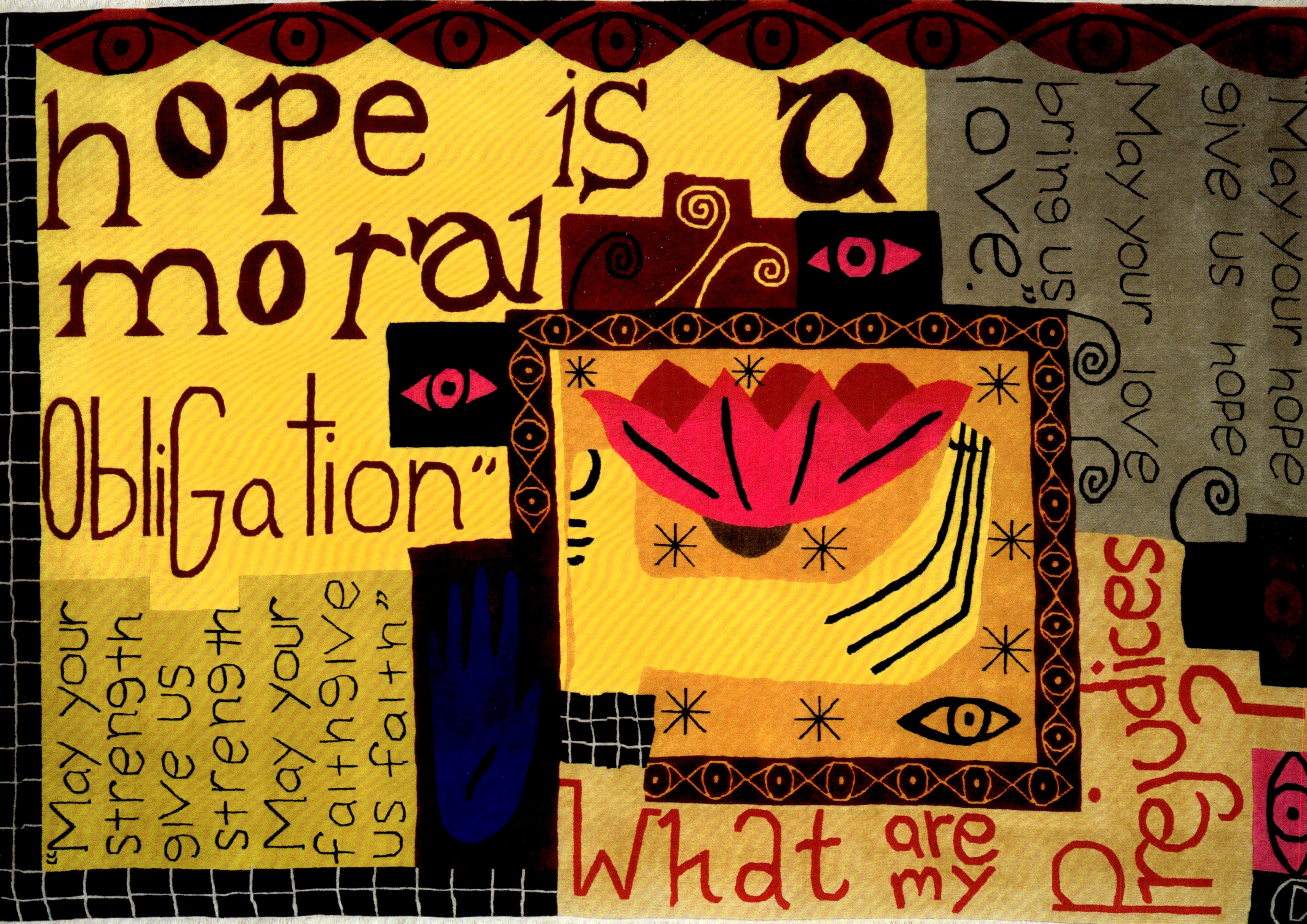
hope is a moral obligation"
"May your strength give us strength May your faith give us faith"
What are my prejudices?
"May your hope give us hope
May your love bring us love."

Essay by Lisa van Doren

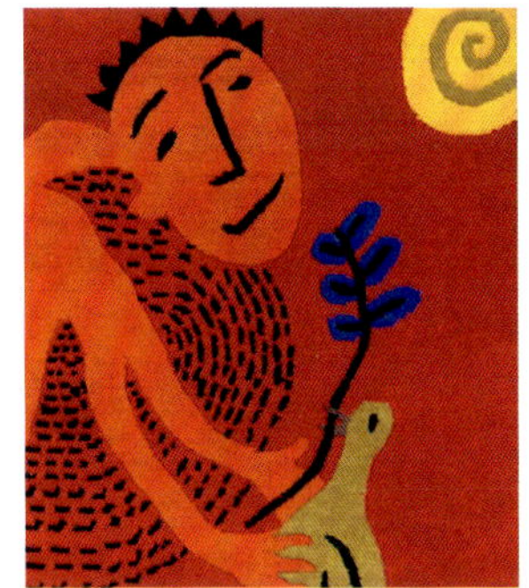

Story Rugs
Tales of Freedom

the work of Dale Gottlieb

Whatcom Museum of History & Art
Bellingham, Washington

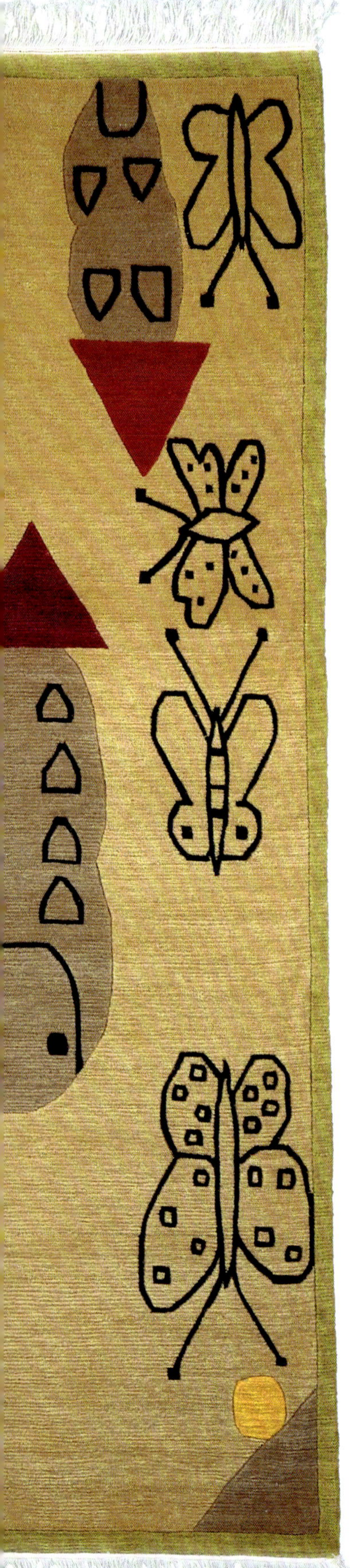

Foreword

presenting the work of a local artist whose process and message so deftly embody our goals of community building is especially rewarding for the staff and board of the Whatcom Museum of History & Art. Weaving together art, community, literacy, and multiculturalism, *Story Rugs—Tales of Freedom: The Work of Dale Gottlieb* offers viewers many opportunities to explore important issues of equality and diversity. Promoting peaceful coexistence among diverse cultures is a lofty goal, and Gottlieb's lifelong commitment to humanitarianism is clear in the stories she tells in brightly colored wool. As a community resource, the Whatcom Museum strives to promote these same ideas of acceptance and hope.

Gottlieb's work is very much about collaboration and cooperation, and this exhibition and accompanying catalogue would not have been possible without the help of many key people. First, I would like to express our sincerest appreciation to the collectors who generously lent their rugs and paintings to the exhibition. Their participation enabled us to present this unique selection of artworks, which so aptly represents Gottlieb's focus and passion.

The exhibition is sponsored by The Starbucks Foundation, Peoples Bank, the Southern Poverty Law Center, and the Community Food Co-op, with additional support provided by the City of Bellingham, Washington State Arts Commission, and the National Endowment for the Arts. We are enormously grateful to these sponsors for their generosity and commitment to the arts. In addition, we are deeply indebted to the numerous contributors to this catalogue, who are specifically thanked on page 62 of this book. Most notably, Linda Gardner of Lucia Douglas Gallery provided crucial fund-raising assistance. These individuals possess a resolute belief in Gottlieb and her work, and their support enabled us to create this important and lasting record of the exhibition.

The many talents of the staff at the Whatcom Museum were also crucial to the project. I would like to thank our Curator of Art, Lisa Van Doren, who has gently led the exhibition to a successful conclusion. Lisa convinced me early on that Gottlieb's work was deserving of an exhibition, a fact that was cemented the first time I saw the artist's textiles in person. Also essential were the fund-raising skills of Kathleen Iwersen, whose contagious enthusiasm for this project engendered the broad base of support it received. As always, Scott Wallin provided an excellent exhibition design, which was accomplished with care and ingenuity by the installation crew. Thanks also to Mary Jo Maute for initially recommending Gottlieb for an exhibition, and to Deanna Zipp, whose amazing organizational skills helped keep the exhibition and catalogue planning on track. In addition, we extend our appreciation to our local Starbucks representative, Dee Wiest, for the enthusiasm and energy she has dedicated to this project.

We are fortunate to have worked with Ed Marquand and the talented staff at Marquand Books, whose respect for and advocacy of artists are truly inspiring. In particular, we acknowledge John Hubbard for his insightful, sensitive design of this beautiful catalogue, and Jennifer Sugden for her skillful management of the publication.

Finally, our heartfelt thanks go to Dale Gottlieb herself for the depth of time and consideration she has given to this project. We are fortunate to have her as our friend and neighbor, and as an artist active in our local community. The intelligence and sensitivity inherent in her work speak to its lasting quality, and she makes our world a more colorful and hopeful place through the stories she tells.

Thomas A. Livesay, Director
Whatcom Museum of History & Art

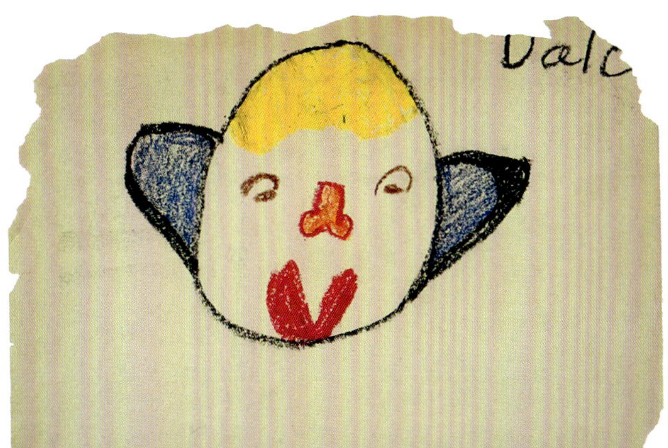

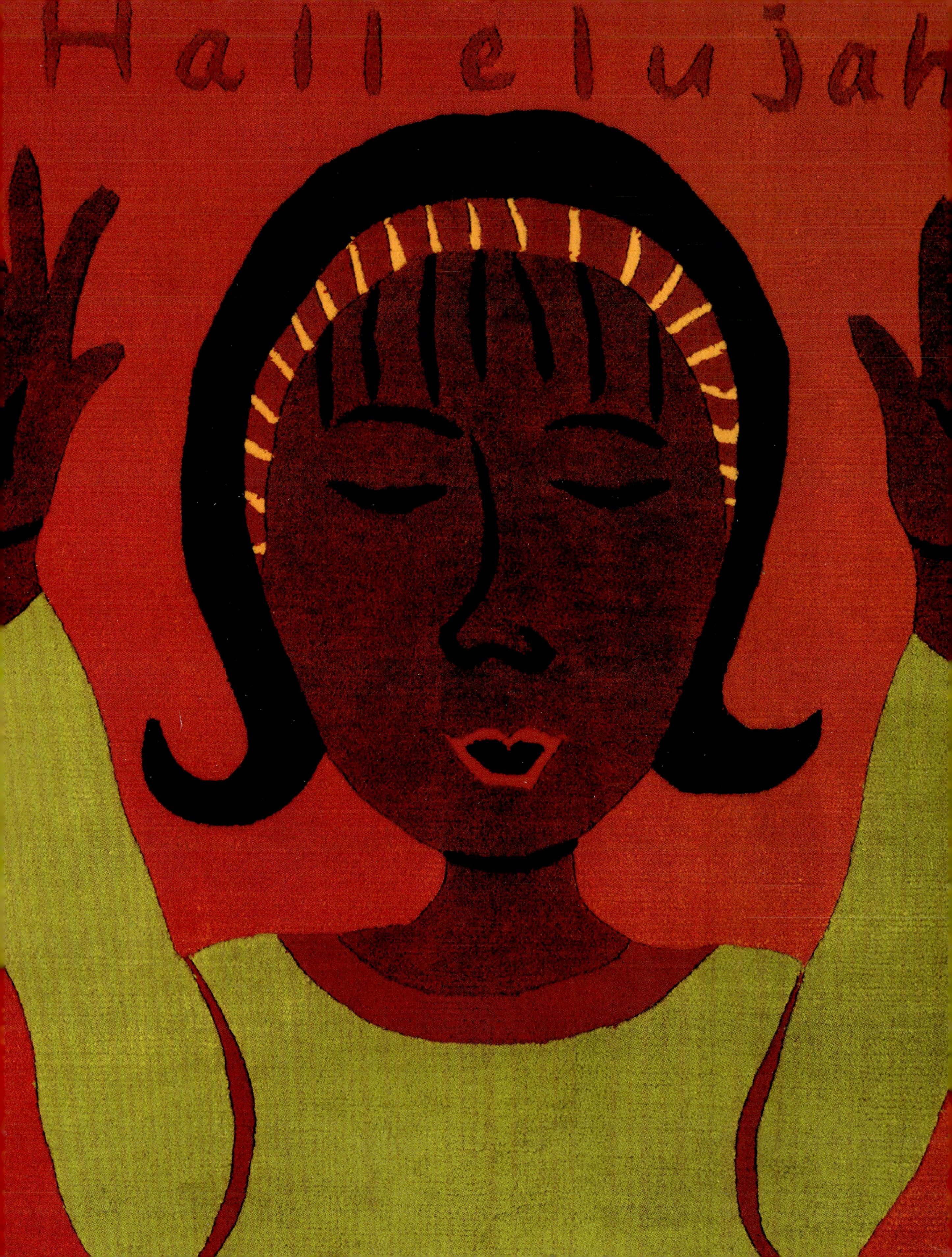
Hallelujah

Story Rugs
Tales of Freedom

by Lisa Van Doren

As you walk up the steps to Dale Gottlieb's studio, it becomes clear that you are in for an unusual experience. A window in the door is etched with an all-seeing eye and the words "To see I need thee." Stepping inside, you are greeted with an abundance of color, carefully mixed and chosen by someone who speaks its language fluently. The walls and window ledges are adorned with an array of carved and painted sacred art from a multitude of sources. A Balinese wooden angel stands guard above the door, while a beaded African sun, various *milagros,* and an old Mexican *retablo* all promote spiritual and physical health as well as artistic inspiration. A portrait of the artist wearing a halo, painted by a friend, hangs near the bookshelves, and just around the corner is a photograph of three Haitian women enacting a voodoo ceremony. This diverse mix of sacred figures, representing a world of stories and viewpoints, all comfortably coexist in Gottlieb's creative space. Her studio is representative of her life and her art: a blend of compelling ideas, serious spirituality, joyous color, humor, sorrow, and gratitude.

Gottlieb's art is inspired by the stories of humanity. She is especially drawn to people who have faced seemingly insurmountable obstacles of discrimination and oppression. The events in these people's lives, including their struggles to confront injustice and their pursuits of freedom—personal, spiritual, and political—provide her with a creative impetus that infuses, and extends beyond, all aspects of her life and artwork. The stories of Holocaust victims, civil-rights activists, and homeless self-taught artists might not seem compatible with the transcendent colors and bold lines that Gottlieb employs in her rugs, but she is able to balance a delicate symmetry of joy and sorrow, hope and tragedy. She embarks on a risky venture, but her methods are surprisingly effective: the playful-looking compositions draw you in, and the

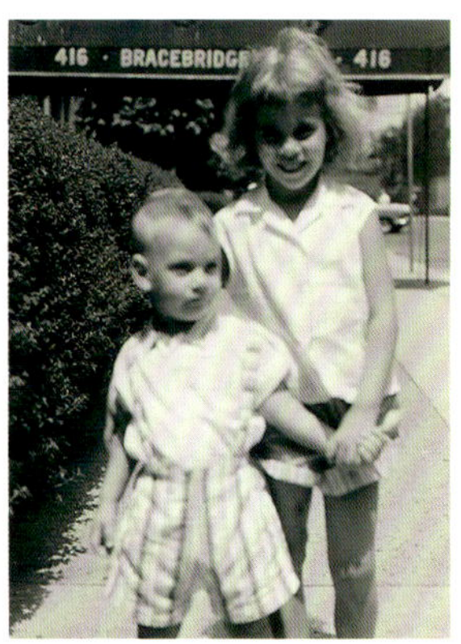

compelling, serious stories behind the designs keep you there.

She has pursued her vision for years, with determination and optimism. Her commitment to telling these tales of freedom and her hope regarding human potential have influences that can be traced back to her childhood. Gottlieb was raised during the 1950s in a large Brooklyn apartment building alongside her Jewish grandparents, aunts, uncles, and cousins. Growing up in this close-knit, diverse neighborhood, she was surrounded by people of varied races, religious beliefs, and sexual orientations. The multitude of languages, customs, and cultures she encountered daily as a child gave her an early and deep understanding of the importance of diversity.

Equality and a sense of moral justice were ingrained in her from a very early age. She attended Brooklyn's Ethical Culture School through the eighth grade. This unique school follows an unconventional path, adhering to a firm basis in philosophy and humanitarianism. According to the artist, "Being a goody-goody was frowned upon. Being brave enough to say what you believed was rewarded." Every race, class, and cultural background was embraced, and students attended ethics class twice a week. The school was a haven for a creative, thoughtful child such as Dale, whose mother, Zelda, dubbed her a "head spinner" because of her ceaseless curiosity and inquisitiveness. The artist adds, "My mother kept an ongoing numerical record of the Excedrin headaches I had given her."[1]

Gottlieb knew from a very early age that she would be an artist and even predicted in her high school newspaper that she would write and illustrate children's books (to date, she has written and/or illustrated twenty-one). This early interest in storytelling and the narrative potential of art has remained constant throughout her career. Equally important is the artist's unswerving belief in art's healing and transformative powers. When she was twenty, Gottlieb interrupted her studies at the School of Art and Design at Alfred

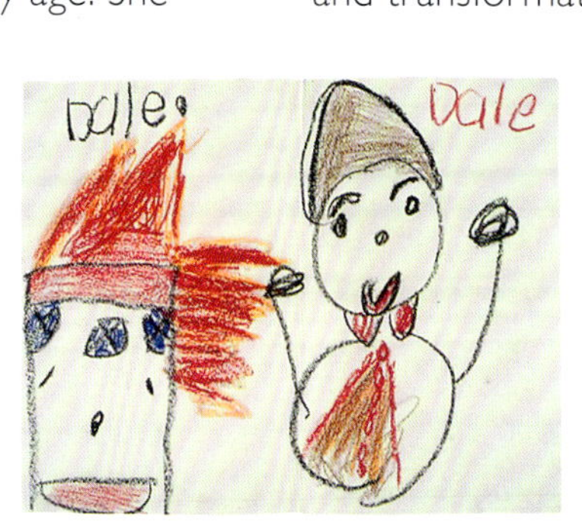

University in western New York for a sojourn in India at a Hindu ashram. A spiritual seeker all her life, she was moved by the rituals and meditative technique she learned in India and seriously considered dropping out of art school to lead an ascetic life. She came to realize that she was forcing this new direction, and that her true path involved creating art. Several months later she returned to art school and graduated with honors for outstanding work. "Gratefully, I realized that I didn't have to stop doing what I loved the most in order to grow spiritually," reflects the artist. The creation of her art is a crucial aspect of this search for self-awareness and spiritual growth.

Gottlieb spent many years painting and drawing, developing and refining her artistic style. In the early 1990s, she began to think about expanding her paintings into another medium and forged a relationship with Lobsang Tenzing, a Tibetan Buddhist who lives and works with his family in Nepal. Followers of the Dalai Lama, his parents fled Tibet after the Chinese invasion and settled in Nepal in 1960, where they started the carpet business that Lobsang now operates. All of Lobsang's looms are certified with Rugmark, a global nonprofit organization working to end child labor and offering educational opportunities to children in India, Nepal, and Pakistan.[2]

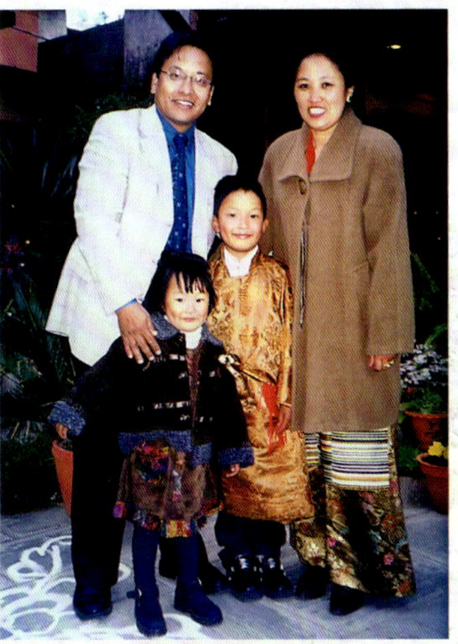

This collaboration with Lobsang, which began in 1993, is both philosophically and artistically significant to the artist. She finds the relationship mutually beneficial, allowing her to explore a new medium and helping Lobsang's family by providing business. The product of their joint labor feeds both of their families. Gottlieb feels a strong connection with the weavers and sees similarities between the Tibetan people's struggle for freedom from the Chinese and the history of oppression in her own Jewish heritage.

She is genuinely amazed by the rug-making process and by how smoothly the production goes, especially considering that the key players are thousands of miles apart. In Bellingham, Gottlieb creates a gouache painting that serves as the rug design. She mixes her paints to match the color-coded yarns Lobsang uses and indicates on a digital scan of the painting the numbers of the corresponding yarn colors. She e-mails a picture of the color-coded design to Lobsang, and his weavers create a proportional

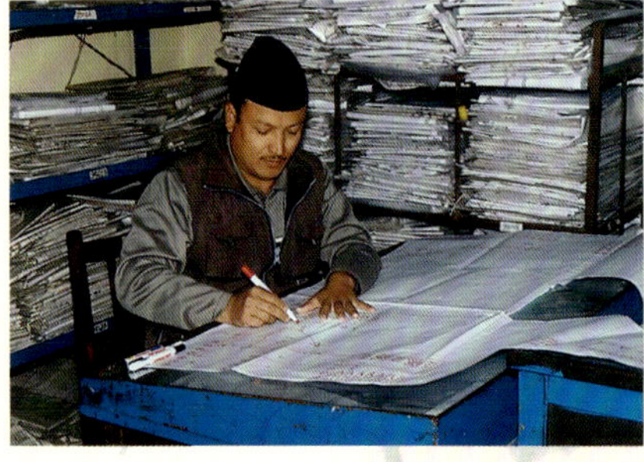

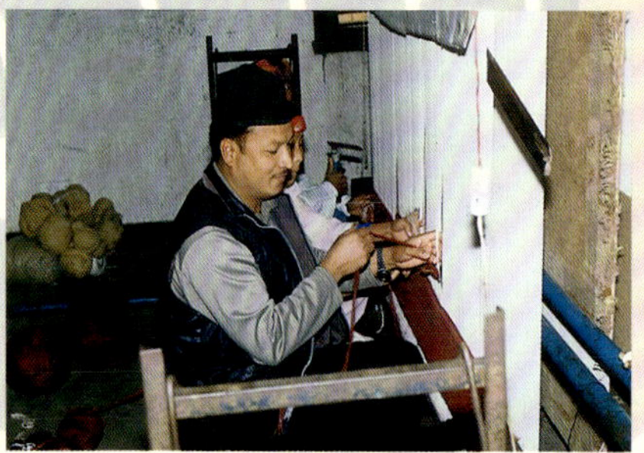

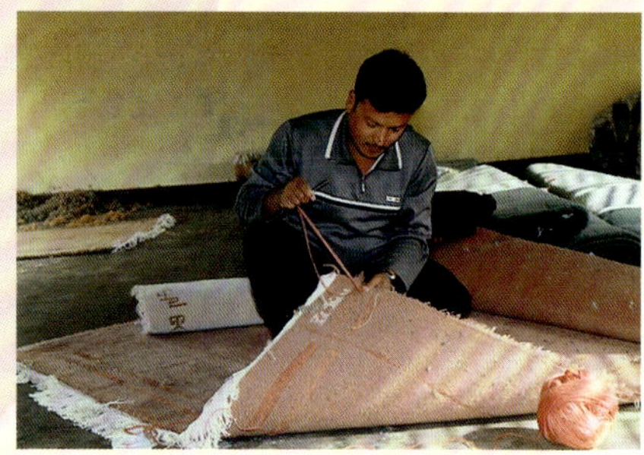

grid from which they weave the rug. Each rug is hand-knotted, using hand-spun and hand-dyed wool, with at least eighty knots per square inch. This labor-intensive process ensures a beautiful, consistent design and a thick, luxurious texture.

Roughly three months after sending the design to Nepal, the artist receives the finished rug in the mail. She recalls the experience of viewing her first rug: "It blew my socks off! I thought they were wizards—it was so beautiful . . . When you know that you're looking at eighty knots per square inch, and then you look at how large an eight-by-ten-foot rug is, it's amazing to realize the effort and skill that's gone into it. These people are experts at what they do." Even ten years after receiving that first shipment, it still feels, each time, like she has been given a gift.

The new medium transformed the substance of Gottlieb's artistic expression. Whereas a painting's content and imagery rest on the

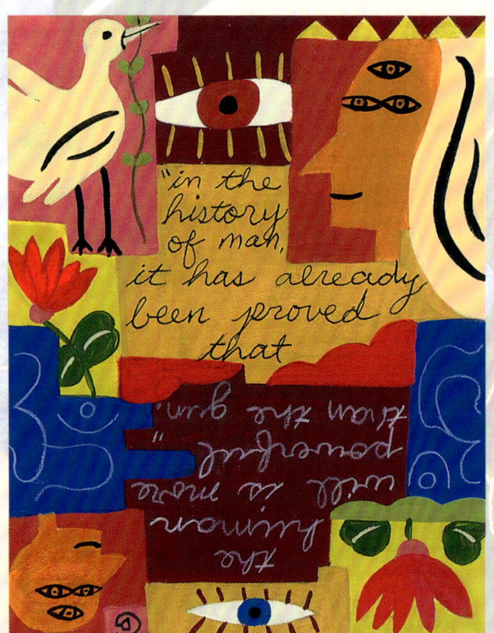

His Holiness the Dalai Lama, 2003

I've always wanted to do a portrait of the Dalai Lama, but my collaborator, Lobsang Tenzing, says Tibetan Buddhists aren't allowed to create images of His Holiness. Quoting the Dalai Lama is, of course, permitted. His words are timeless but simple, bearing wisdom characteristic of the highly evolved. I am inspired by his strength and understanding of true forgiveness.

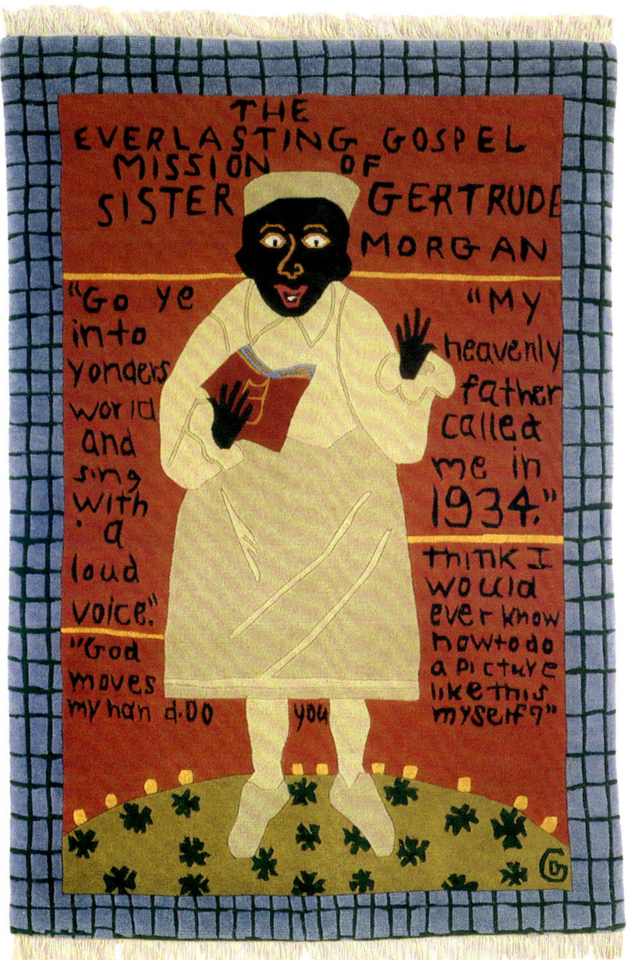

Sister Gertrude Morgan, 1995

Sister Gertrude has inspired me often. Her artworks, writings, and music are always spiritual in nature.

surface of canvas, paper, or panel, the words and images in Gottlieb's rugs make up the weave of the carpet itself. The stories are not superficial, fleeting words or images applied quickly to a surface, but lasting and significant thoughts and remembrances. Each strand of yarn, knotted by hand, makes up a tiny piece not only of the rug as an object but also of the design and the message it conveys. The story depicted is integral to the physical, structural makeup of the rug, reinforcing the strength of its message.

Gottlieb's view of her relationship with the weavers as a true collaboration becomes apparent when she talks about issues of control. When she turns a design over to the weavers, she relinquishes control of the process. This can be an uncomfortable position for an artist—having to entrust a creation to the care of others. The finished rug is usually very close to her original intention, but at times there are differences in the design or color scheme. She embraces these small variations, viewing them as evidence of the weavers' hand in the process. This collaborative and cross-cultural process dovetails with the stories of diversity and equality communicated in her rugs.

Because of her need to create art that conveys these messages, Gottlieb can be called a narrative artist, who by definition provides a visual representation of some kind of story. This tradition reaches back thousands of years and includes such varied works of art as ancient Egyptian tomb murals, illuminated manuscripts from the Middle Ages, and heroic battle-scene paintings by nineteenth-century French masters. In addition to depicting familiar stories, which the viewer recognizes and retells in his or her mind, narrative artists sometimes employ text in their works to illuminate what the picture represents. This is the case with many of the artists whose works inspire Gottlieb, such as the visionary Sister Gertrude Morgan.

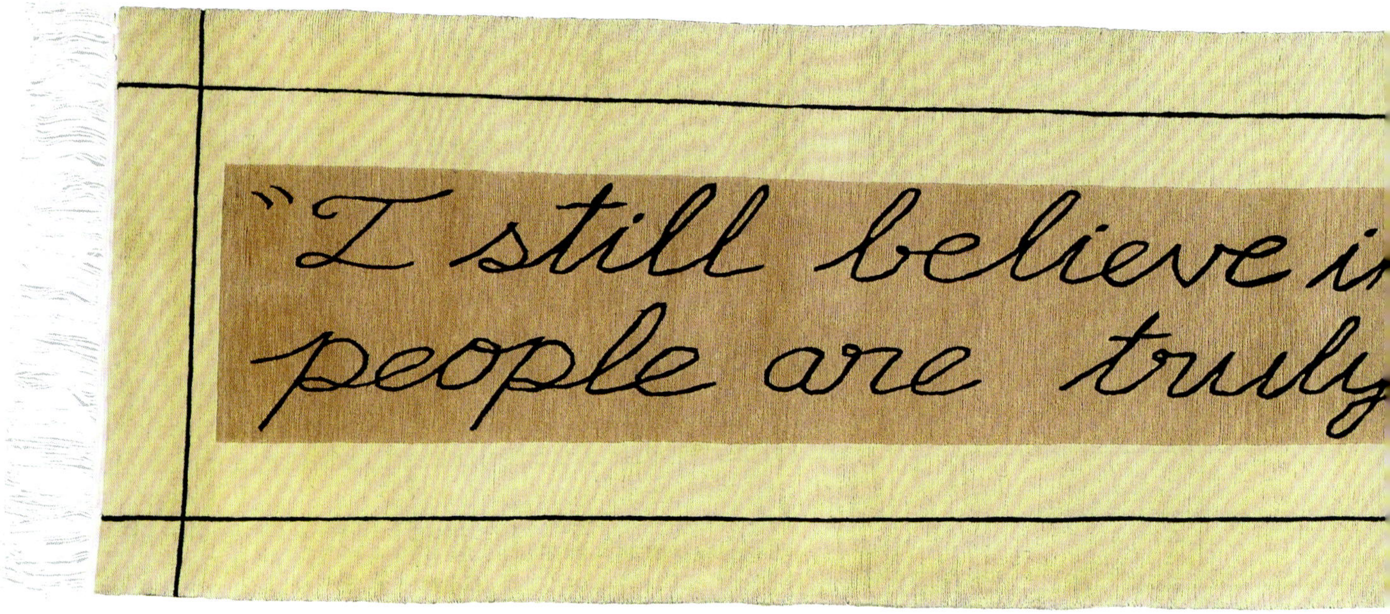

A self-taught artist, Sister Gertrude was called by God to preach the Gospel and she dedicated her life to sharing messages of salvation. Her calling included not only preaching and singing on the streets of New Orleans but also making art to communicate her spiritual mission. Admiring Sister Gertrude's passion as well as her artistic abilities, Gottlieb says, "She's my kind of artist: spiritual, loving, a great painter, and not afraid to cause trouble"—in other words, a kindred spirit. Sister Gertrude painted pictures to illustrate her sermons, often inscribing passages from the Bible or quotations from her own sermons as parts of her compositions. Her narrative technique relied as much on the texts she inscribed as on the images she created. This is a strategy that Gottlieb herself employs.

Words spoken or written by courageous and wise people are particularly important to Gottlieb. Meaningful quotations, phrases, or names are significant to the point that the words and letters themselves appear as key compositional elements in her work. The cursive script appearing in many of the rugs represents the artist's own handwriting, and

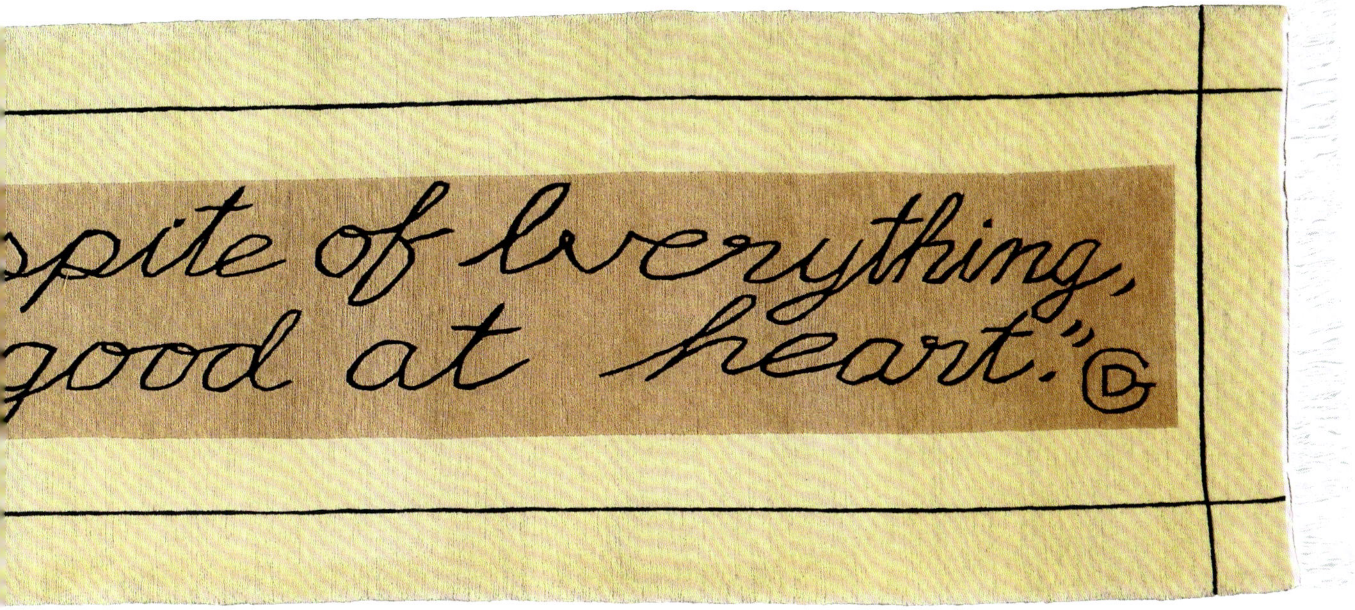

Anne Frank, 2000

These are the words remembered most often from Anne Frank's diary. Unflagging optimism, even in the face of terror.

often the text becomes a focal point in the work, anchoring the figures or, in some cases, taking center stage.

Anne Frank consists entirely of text; no figures, animals, or objects appear in the composition. "I still believe in spite of everything people are truly good at heart" . . . even more than fifty years after these words were written, it is astonishing to read this quote from the diaries of Anne Frank, knowing the horrors she and millions of other Jewish people faced during the Holocaust. Frank's belief in the human potential for self-awareness speaks directly to Gottlieb's own optimism. She sees herself as a midwife, taking this familiar quote and giving it life in a new medium. She embraces the idea that on a rug these words will become part of someone's home in an intimate way—more so than a traditional painting or sculpture because of how the rug will be used. Even if that person is not consciously aware of reading the text every day, the sheer presence of the words in the hallway, on the wall, under the table, or in the living room infuses the home with the philosophy of the quote. This simple, forceful rug operates on several levels simultaneously: it stands on its own as a powerful quotation, causing us to reflect on what we know about the Holocaust; it is visually appealing as an elegant composition made up of swirling, graceful script; and perhaps most

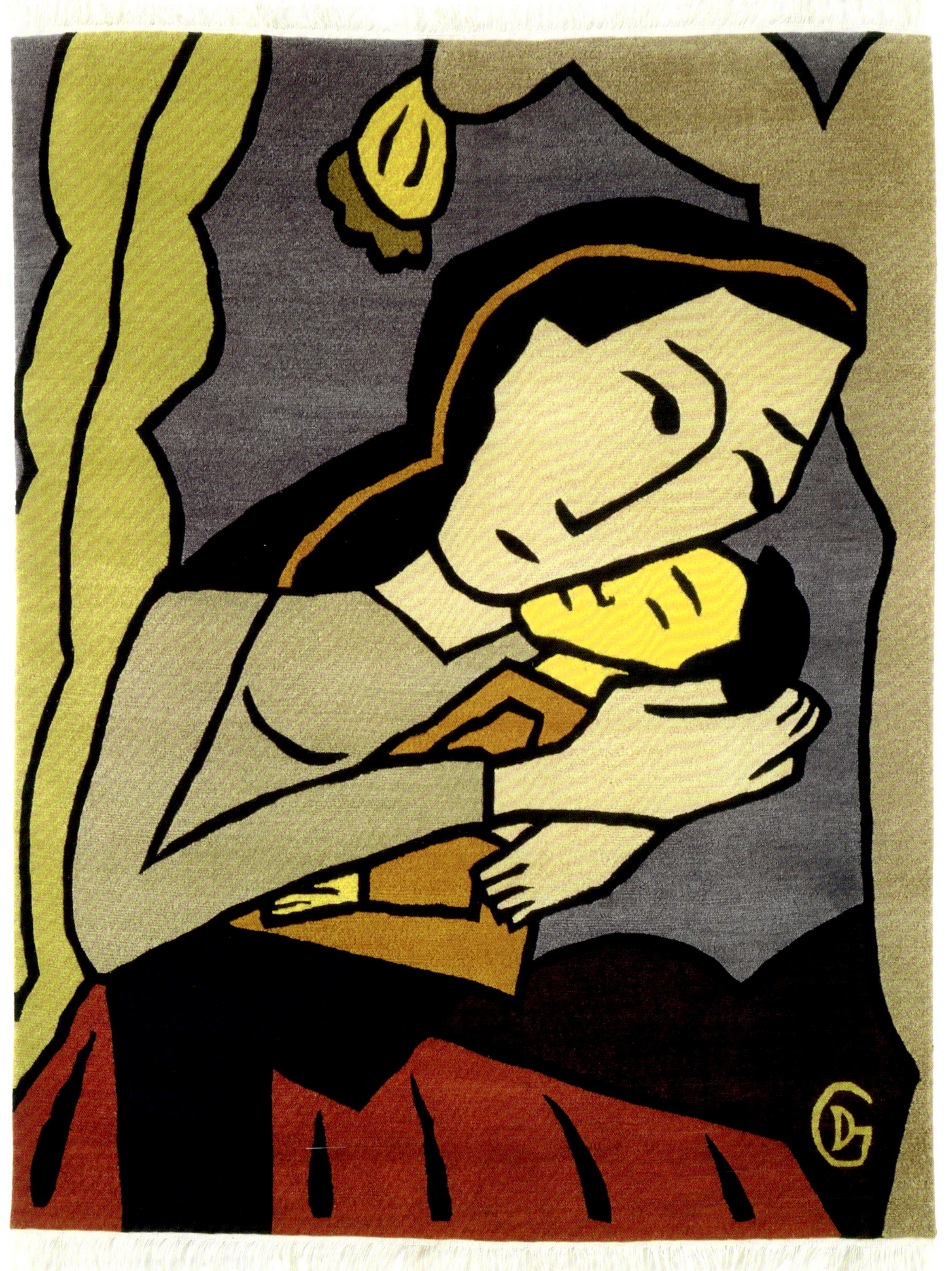

Gathering Strength, 2002

A mother and a child rest after escaping, during the night, from a concentration camp.

important, it serves as an appeal for faith and optimism, qualities embodied by Anne Frank. The rug's success on all three levels is a testament to the effectiveness of Gottlieb's narrative powers.

Although text and words are key elements in many of her compositions, some rugs contain no legible script describing what is depicted and instead employ strong graphic imagery that invites a narrative interpretation. This interpretation is varied, at times informed by our own personal experiences but also affected by shared cultural history—our inherent understanding of significant historical events. In *Gathering Strength,* a mother and child pause after having escaped from a concentration camp. They rest not only to regain physical stamina but also to draw from each other spiritual strength. The three rugs in the *Happy Series,* created in response to the tragedies of September 11, 2001, show neighbors cheerfully greeting one another on a breezy, sunny day. The artist invites us to acknowledge the strength we can find in others and to share in her faith for a better future. She sees treating one another gently and kindly as a vital first step, and her creations are an effort to start the healing process for a spiritually wounded community.

Though most of Gottlieb's rugs tell the stories of people she has admired but never met, she has also created work with unanticipated,

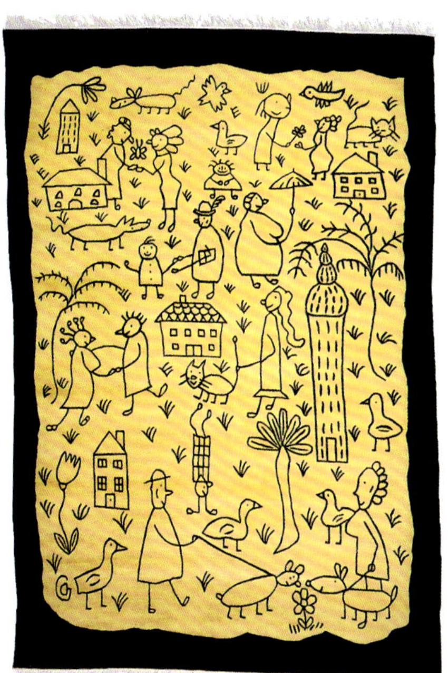

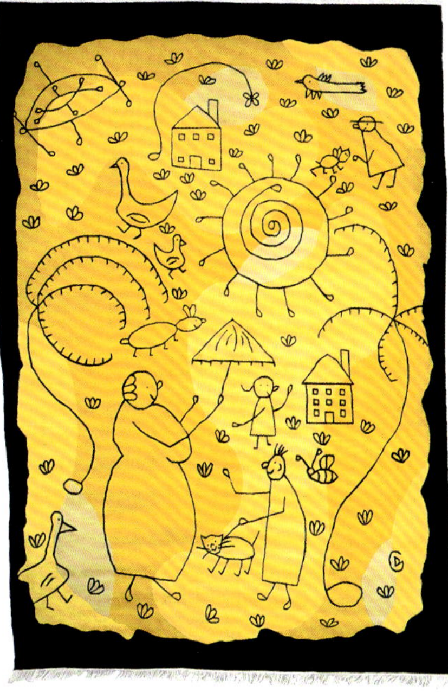

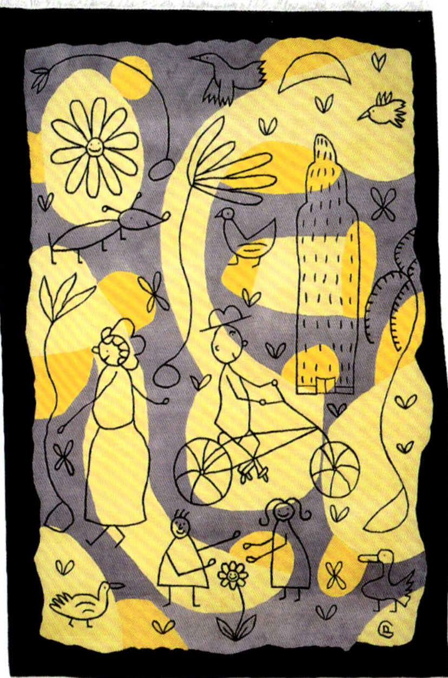

Happier Times, Happy Times, and More Happy Times, all 2002

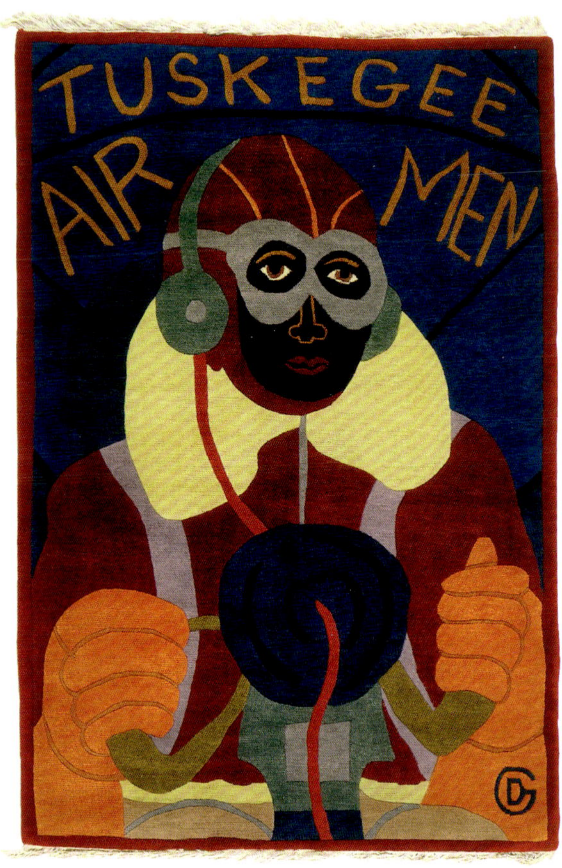

Tuskegee Airmen, 1995

This is an homage to the first black escort pilots in World War II, who fought prejudice here at home while protecting white pilots' planes from being shot down in battle.

profound personal connections, as in *Tuskegee Airmen.* After learning about the first black military pilots, who served during World War II, she wanted to pay tribute to the achievements of these brave men. Trained at Tuskegee Army Air Field in Alabama, the airmen played a major role in the Allied victory, saving the lives of hundreds of bomber pilots by flying escort missions. Gottlieb honors their courage and determination in this rug, which features a single pilot at the flight controls. The words "Tuskegee Airmen" float above his head like a halo. She presents a dignified portrait of a man seriously engaged in his work. Unbeknownst to the artist, the father of her sister-in-law Anne-Marie Johnson had been a Tuskegee Airman. The discovery after the fact that she had created a rug honoring a member of her own extended family was an emotional surprise for Gottlieb, and the rug became a treasured gift for Anne-Marie. As she explains, "I'm so proud of my father and proud of his history. The rug helps me stay in contact with him in a strange way. He died in 1987 and I miss him dearly. The rug hangs proudly in our living room. At night, when lit, the rug can be seen from our driveway to the street. The colors are so wonderful and majestic."[3] In this case, Gottlieb's narrative touched her own family in a very poignant way—a tangible example of her vision of the interconnectedness of human relationships. She created the rug to tell the story of the Tuskegee Airmen, honoring their courage in the face of hardship and offering an opportunity for cultural healing. In the process, she was also able to establish a point of connection between Anne-Marie and her father, helping to heal a family member's feelings of loss.

Artworks that deal with such weighty subjects as the Holocaust, slavery, and civil rights can easily become didactic. Gottlieb successfully avoids this disagreeable tendency by addressing these serious issues with a sensitive touch. She draws our attention first to the redemptive side of the story, as difficult as that may be to find, highlighting her characters' courage and tenacity rather than their pain and anguish. Instead of detailing the persecution of Tibetans, Gottlieb offers a powerful statement on nonviolence from the Dalai Lama. And instead of presenting the horrors inmates faced in the concentration camps, Gottlieb interprets the buildings and trees in the artistic style of its child-prisoners, who created art as a way to cope with a terrifying situation.

In addition, Gottlieb uses specific formal techniques to further captivate us with these sometimes heartbreaking stories. She is not concerned with presenting straight optical reality. The truths she seeks are better communicated in a more abstract manner, in the best of modernist traditions. When Gottlieb depicts figures, she places them in the extreme foreground of the composition, front and center, ready to speak directly to the viewer. Her rugs consistently employ a flattened sense of perspective, with broad areas of saturated color that bring to mind the vibrant paper cutouts that Henri Matisse made late in his life. She effectively combines playful, exaggerated features and poses with bold colors, creating an extraordinarily engaging world that beckons us.

In form, her work may resonate with aspects of Western modernism, but in spirit her art has more in common with Ethiopian medicinal scrolls or the Mexican *retablo* hanging in her studio. Religious artworks such as these are often used ritualistically to heal spiritual or physical wounds. They recount both diverse individual stories and concepts of shared history. These sacred creations are vital to the health of the communities from which they come. Gottlieb's art functions in much the same way, presenting inspirational stories of freedom and diversity, and offering us an opportunity to see connections to these tales within our own lives.

1. All statements by the artist are from a series of conversations with the author, March 2003.

2. Rugmark certifies that the rugs are produced without the use of child labor.

3. Anne-Marie Johnson, correspondence with the author, March 27, 2003.

Terezin, 2000

The Terezin concentration camp in Czechoslovakia was filled with gifted Jews whose children's art often incorporated their surroundings. They used art as a means for coping with a horrible situation. This rug is inspired by the children's work.

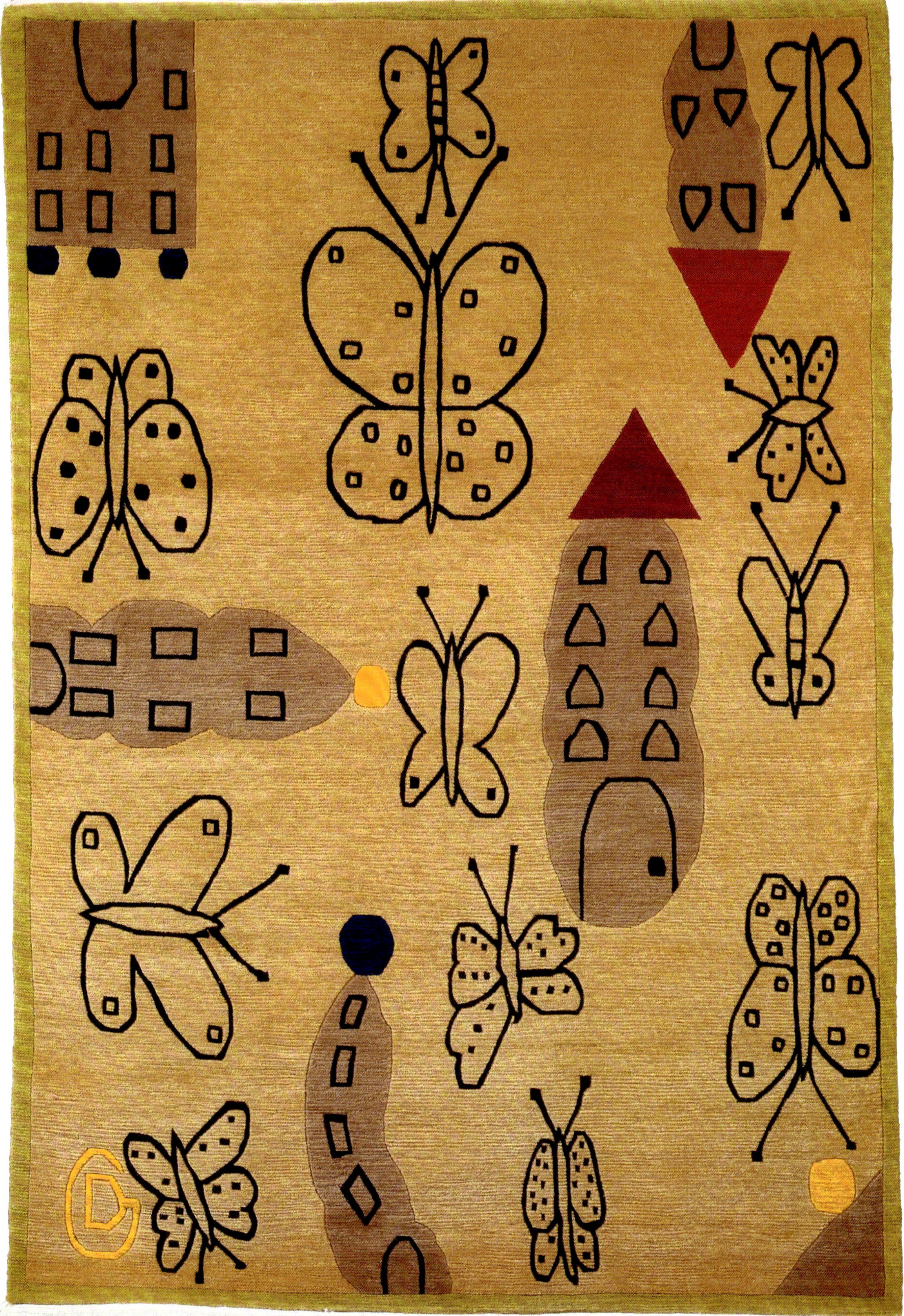

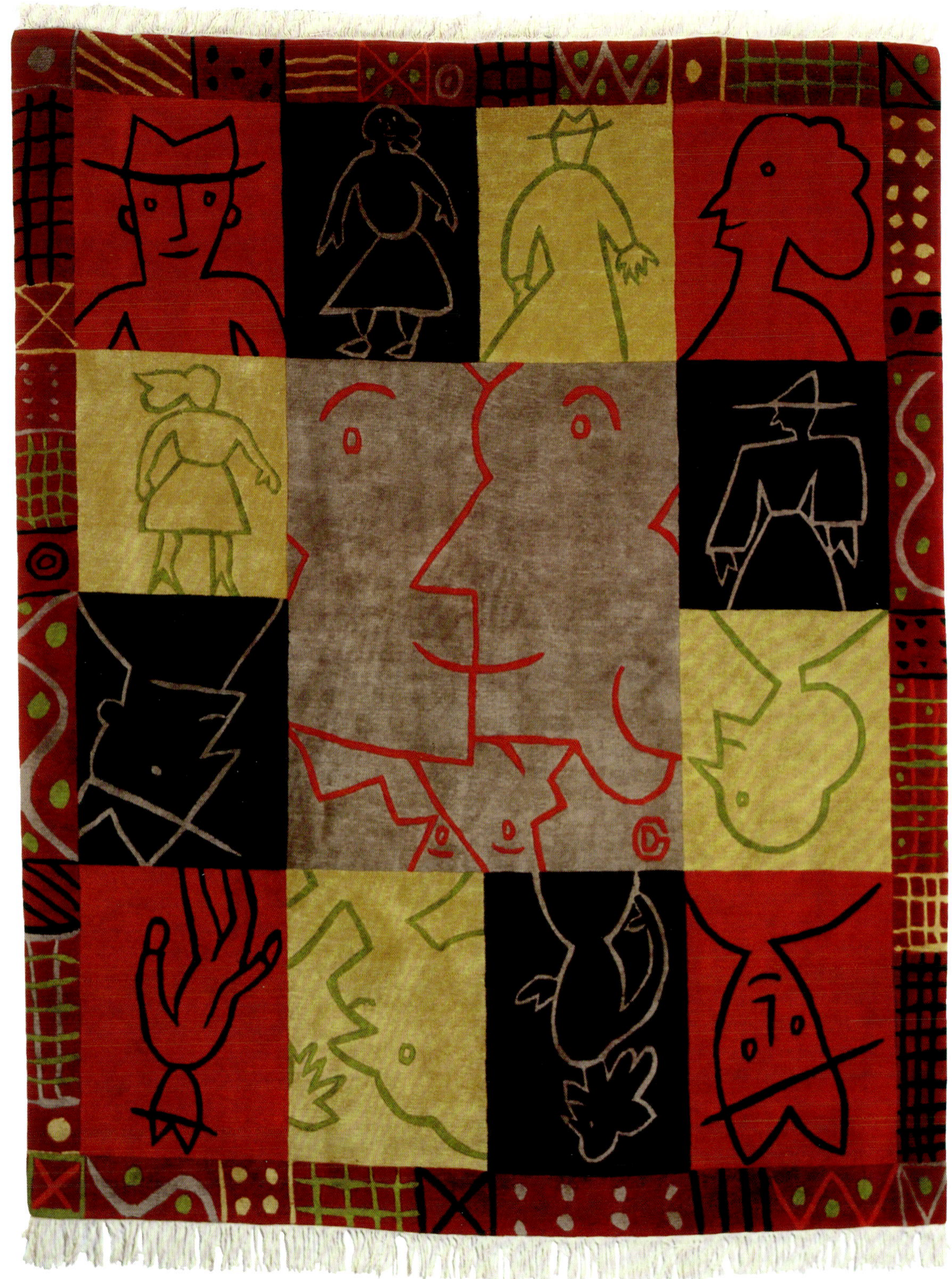

Conversation, 1997

Strangers, family, friends, and foes communicate.

The first step toward respecting our differences.

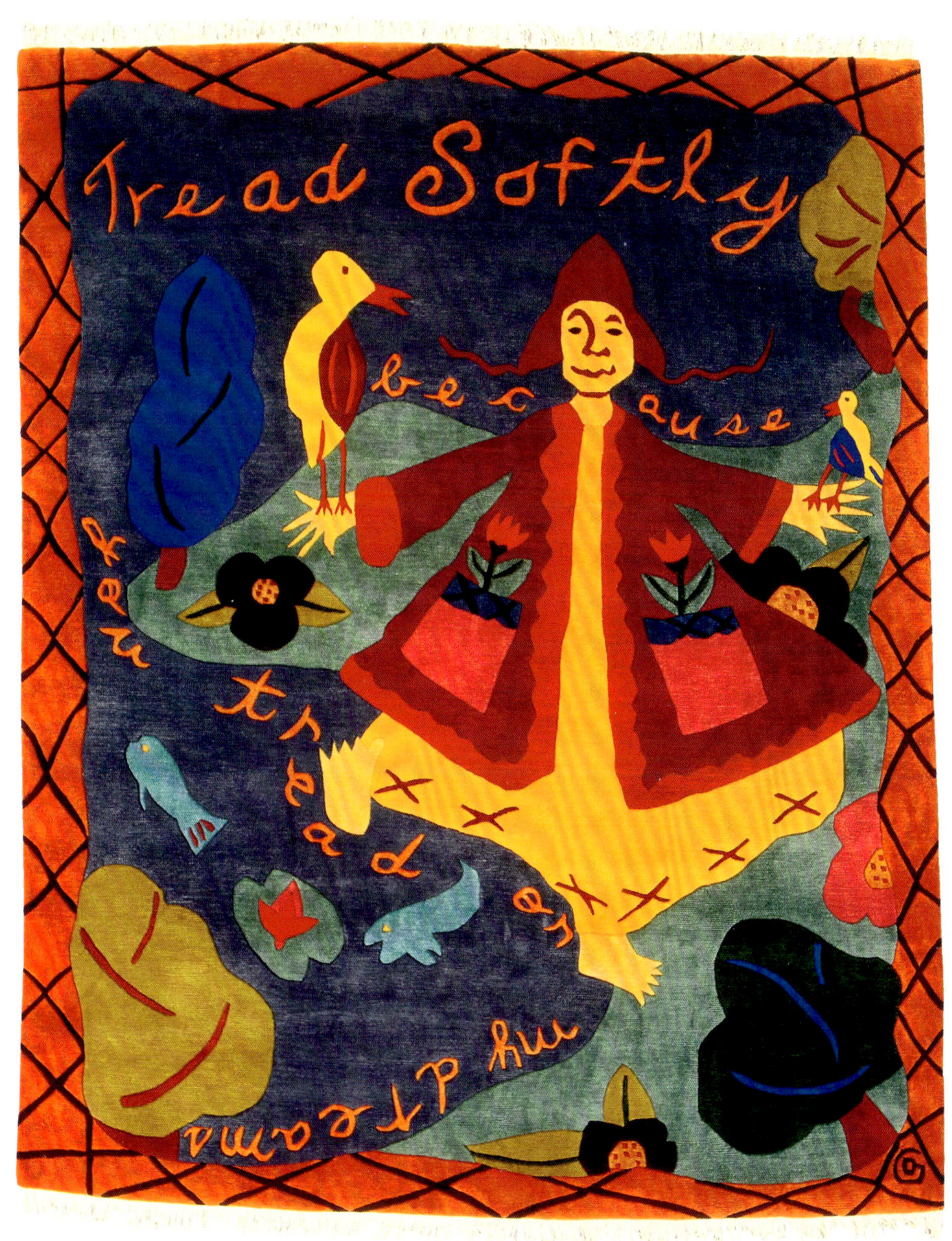

Tread Softly, 1995

The quote used in this rug is the last line of W. B. Yeats's poem "He Wishes for the Cloths of Heaven." A Tibetan Lama walks to freedom.

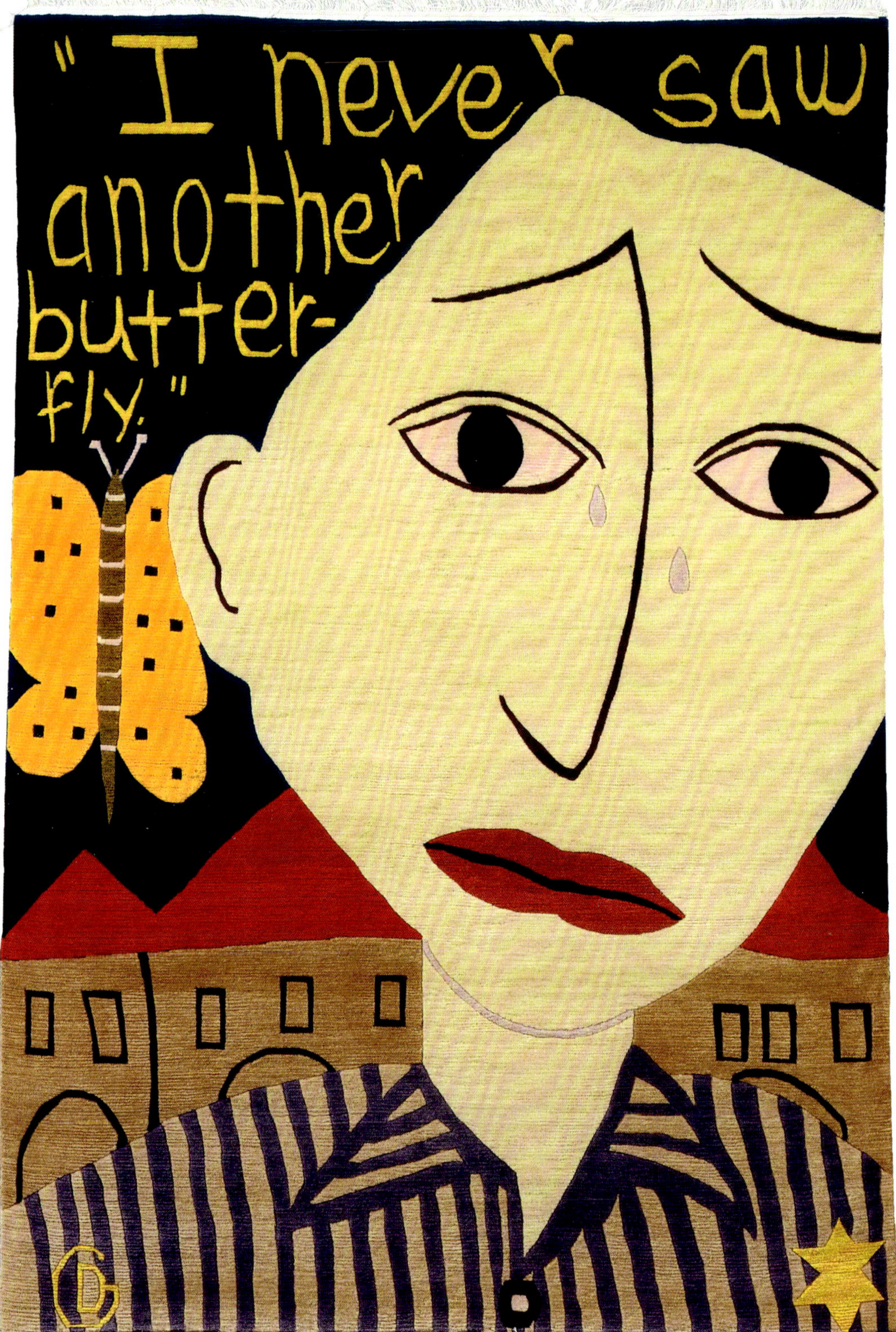
"I never saw
another
butter-
fly."

Pavel Friedman, 2000

Pavel Friedman wrote the poem "I Never Saw Another Butterfly" when he was in the Terezin concentration camp. From there he was sent to Auschwitz and killed. He was fourteen.

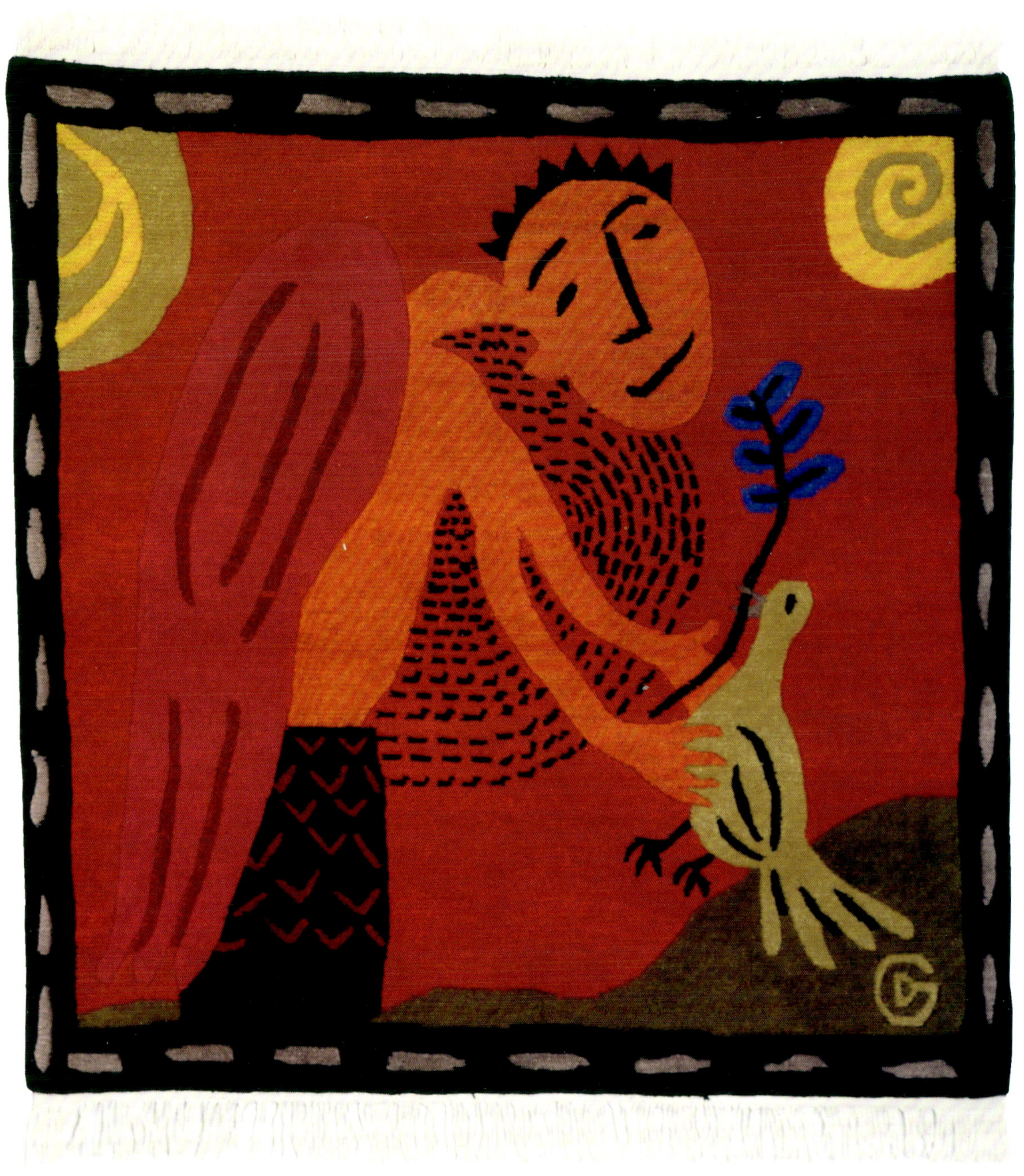

Boy Angel, 1994

Inspired by Haitian voodoo iron art. He has made the transition from mere human to vessel of God.

Hallelujah, 1995

Inspired by African American gospel music.

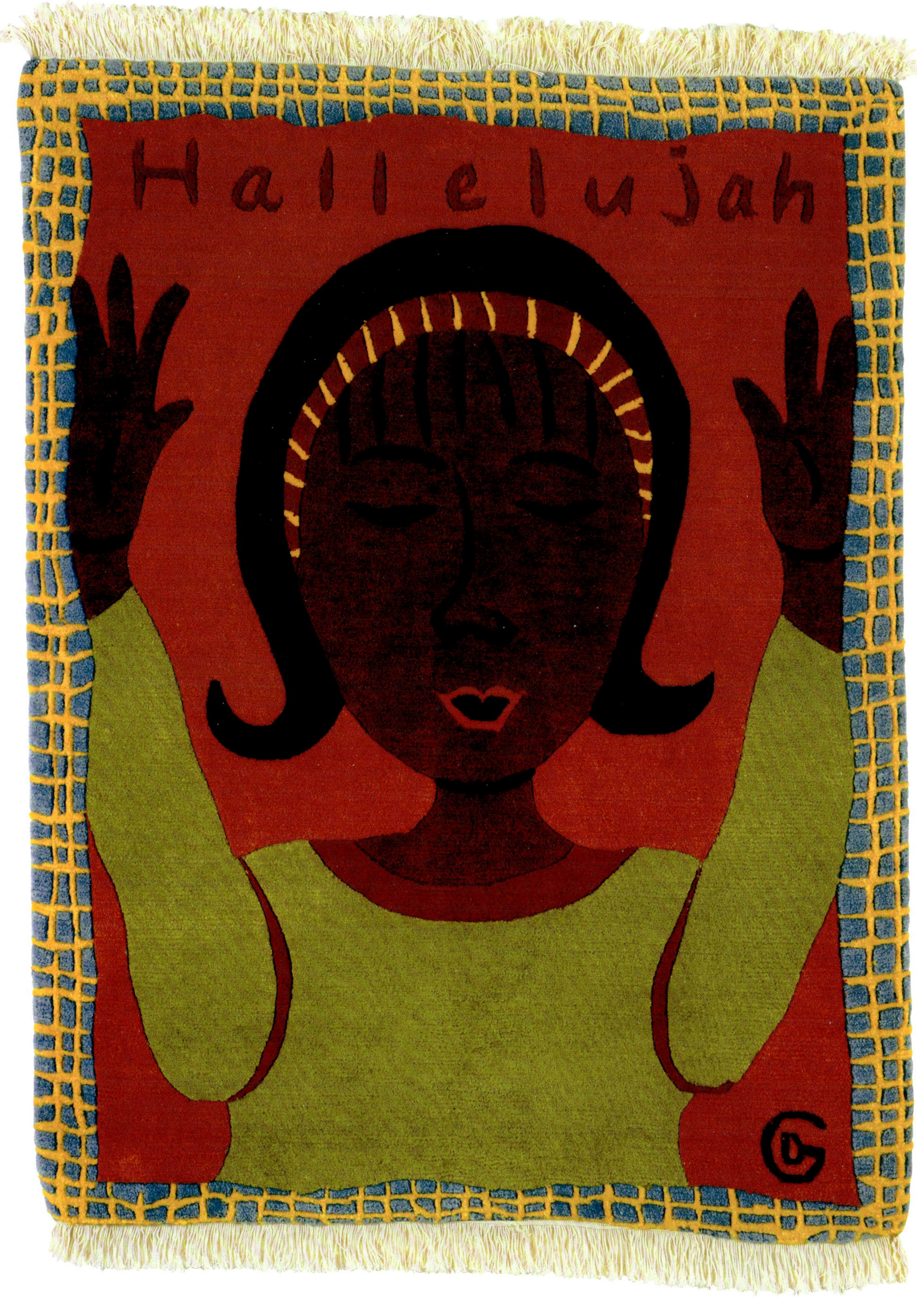

Hallelujah

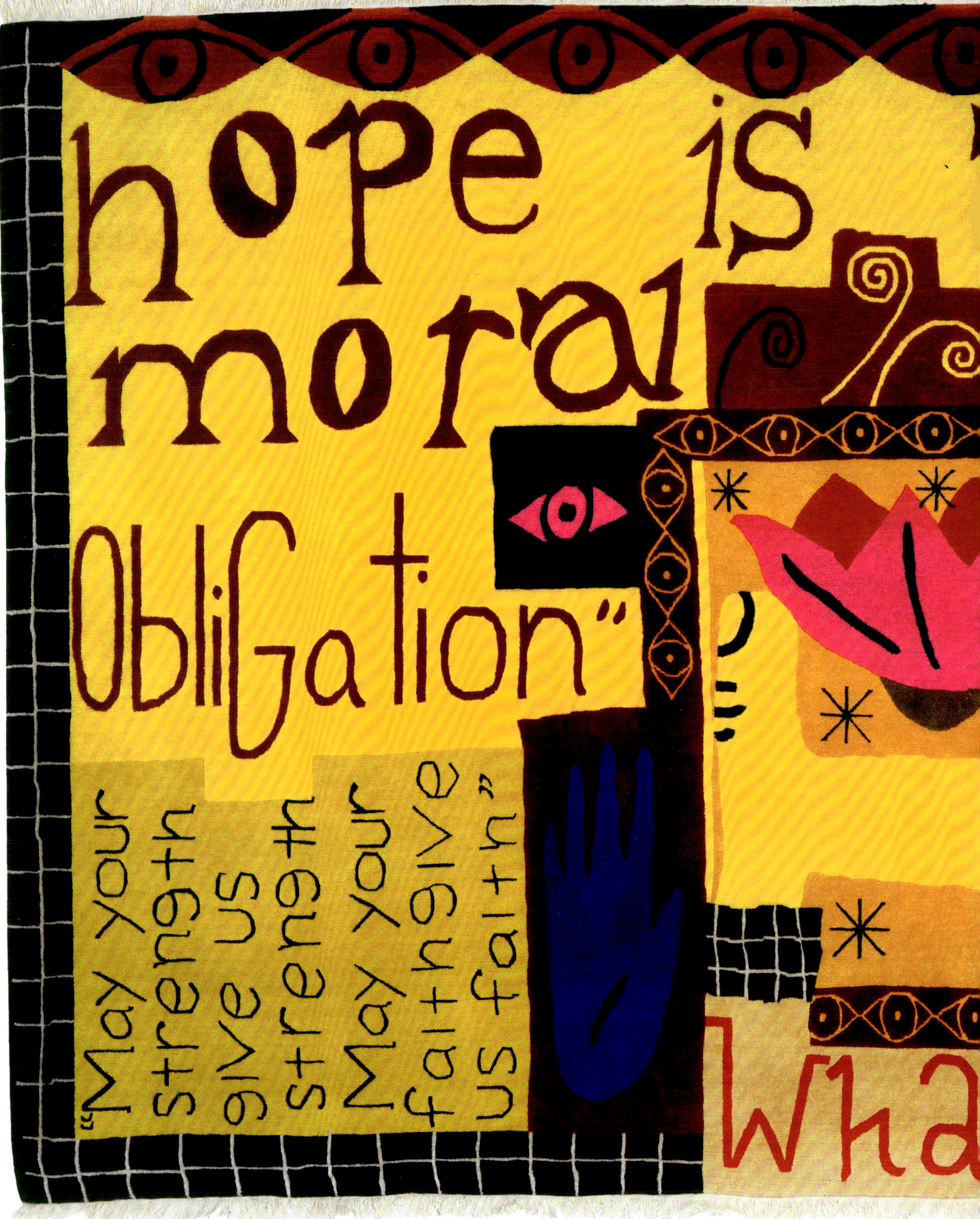
hope is
moral
Obligation"
"May your
strength
give us
strength
May your
faith give
us faith"
Wha

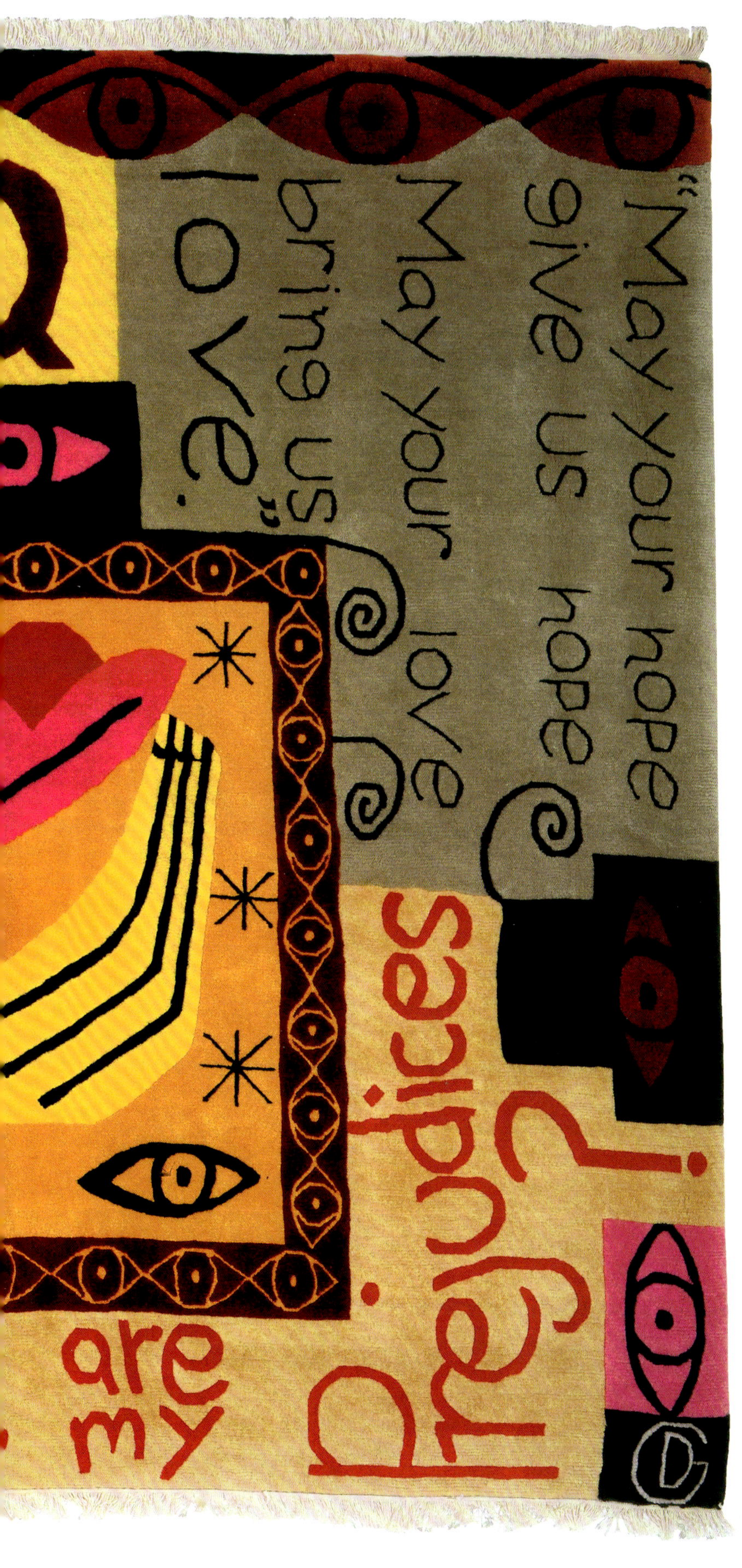

Hope to Change, 2003

My childhood friend Ruth Rachlin told me that Tony Kushner spoke at her daughter's graduation from Vassar last year. I saw his play Angels in America *in Seattle and was moved by his dramatic plea for awareness and compassion regarding AIDS. He implored the class of 2002 to accept the idea that "hope is a moral obligation."*

Bruce Springsteen often inspires me to feel this same obligation. The prayerlike refrain of his song "Into the Fire," from his album The Rising, *written after September 11, 2001, is quoted on both ends of this rug.*

I ask, "What are my prejudices?" so that the viewer and I will answer simultaneously.

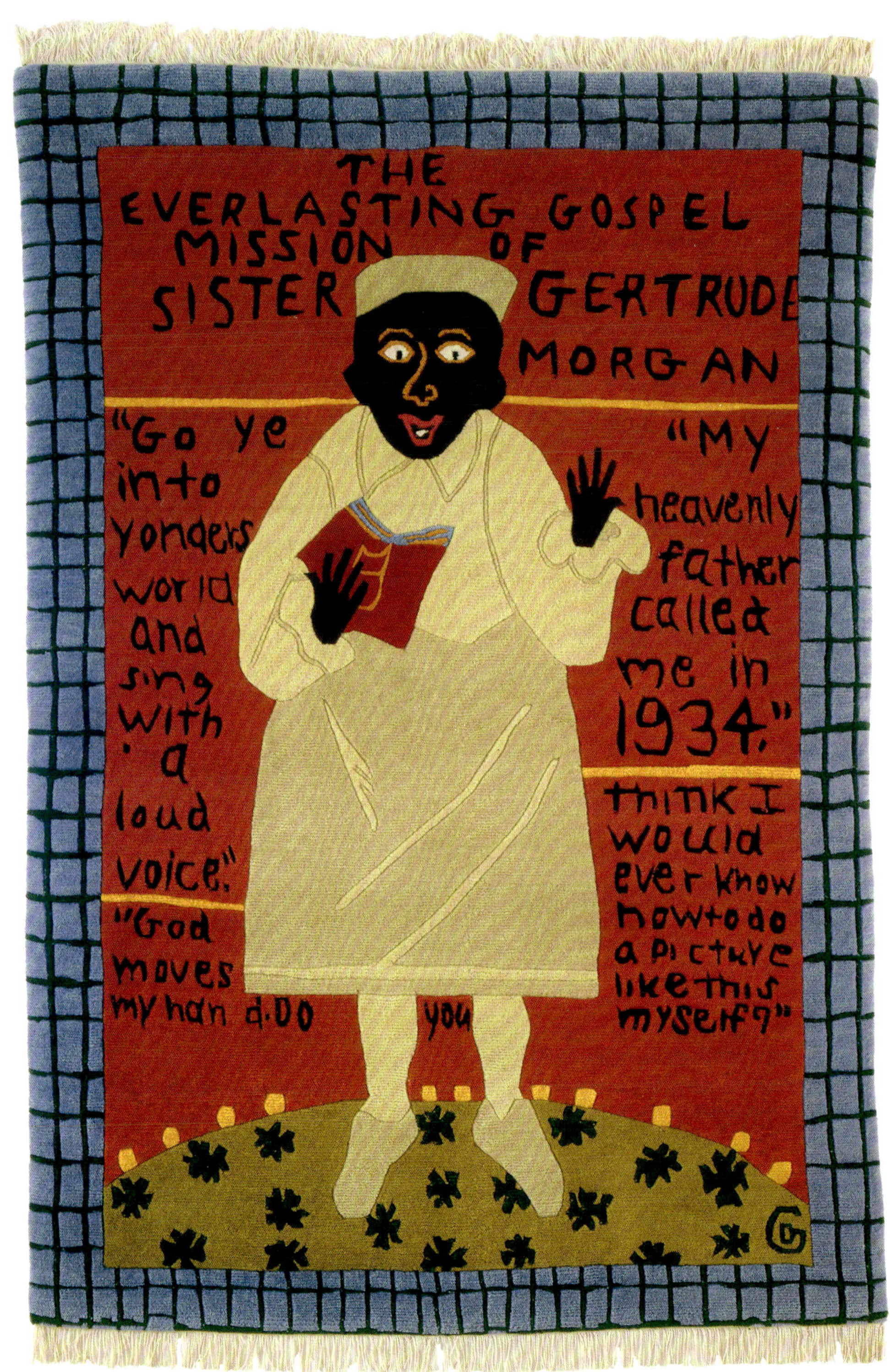

Sister Gertrude Morgan, 1995

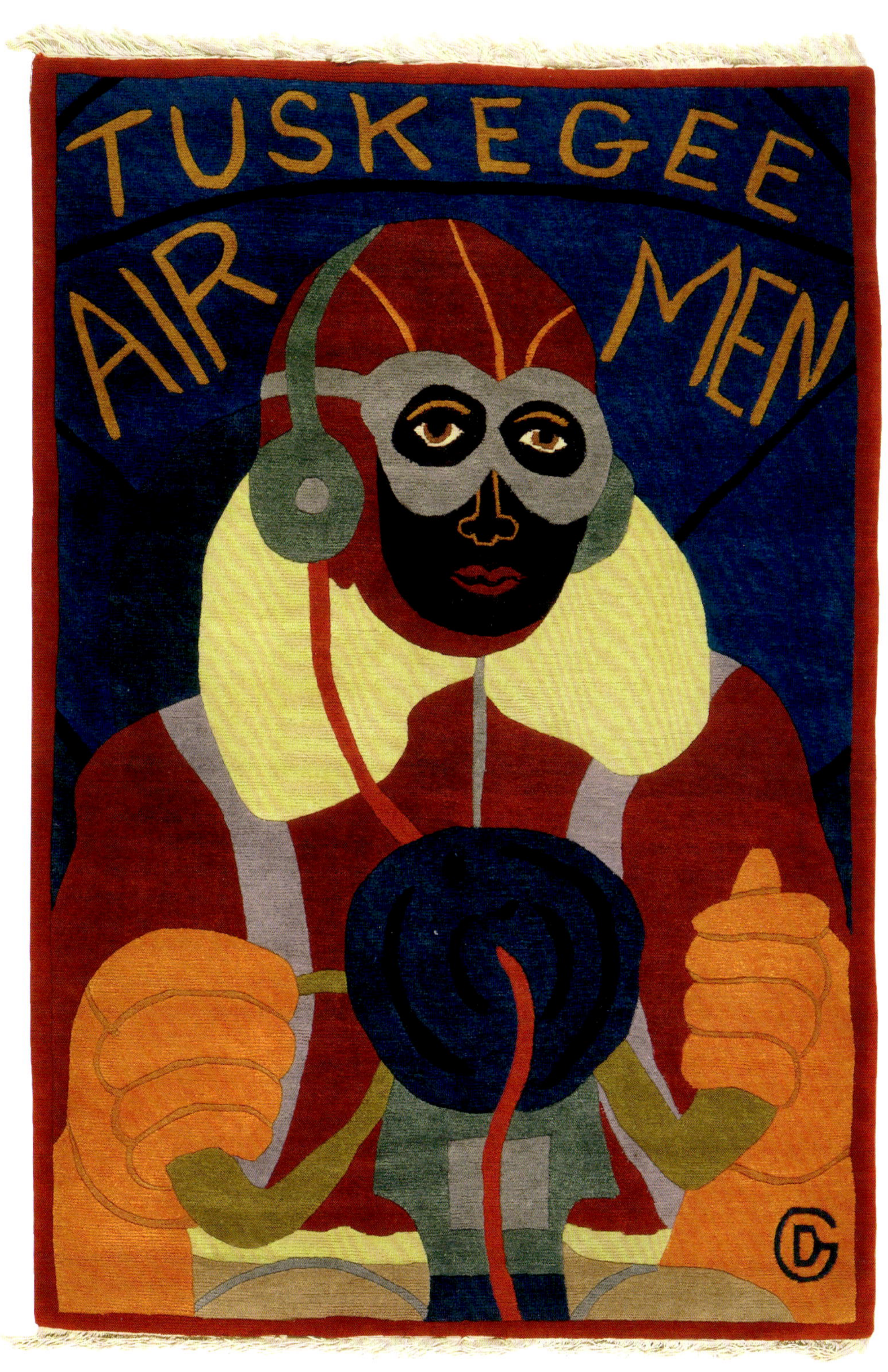

Tuskegee Airmen, 1995

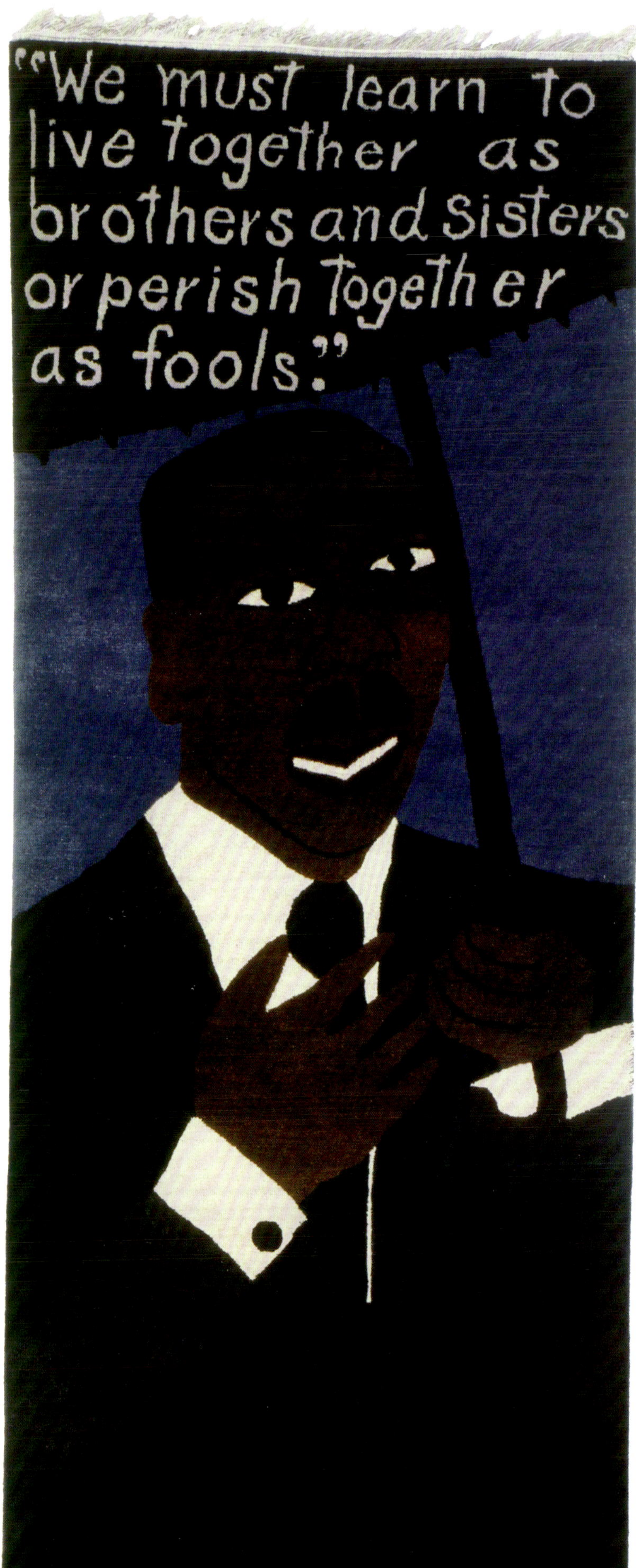

King, 2003

When Martin Luther King Jr. won the Nobel Peace Prize in 1964, he said, in his stirring voice, that the prize was not for just him, but for "all men who love peace and brotherhood." He gave the money to several civil rights groups. King fought hatred through nonviolence, even when standing face-to-face with violent members of the Ku Klux Klan. He never lost faith or hope in human beings. He was the King.

Sojourner Truth, 1994

Sojourner Truth was a courageous abolitionist, suffragette, and feminist.

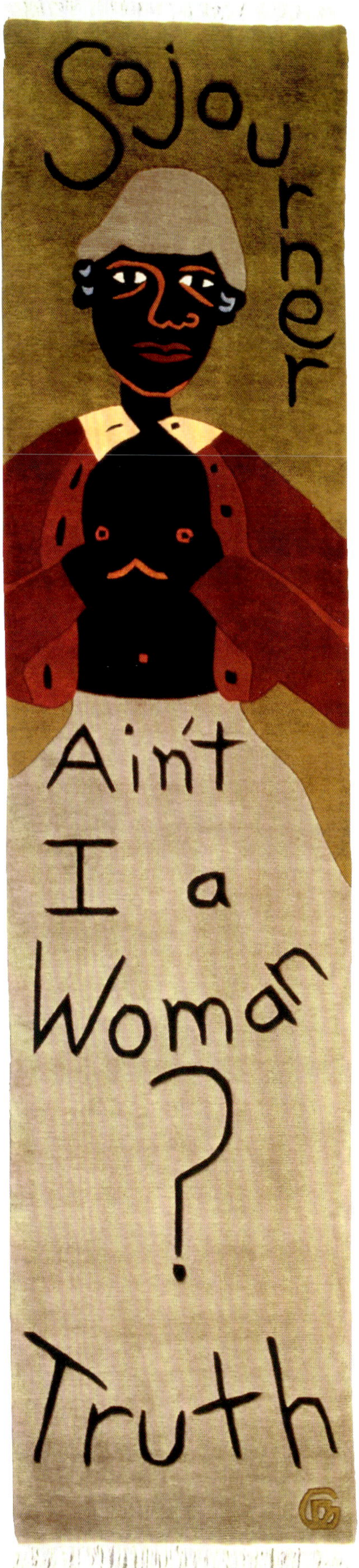

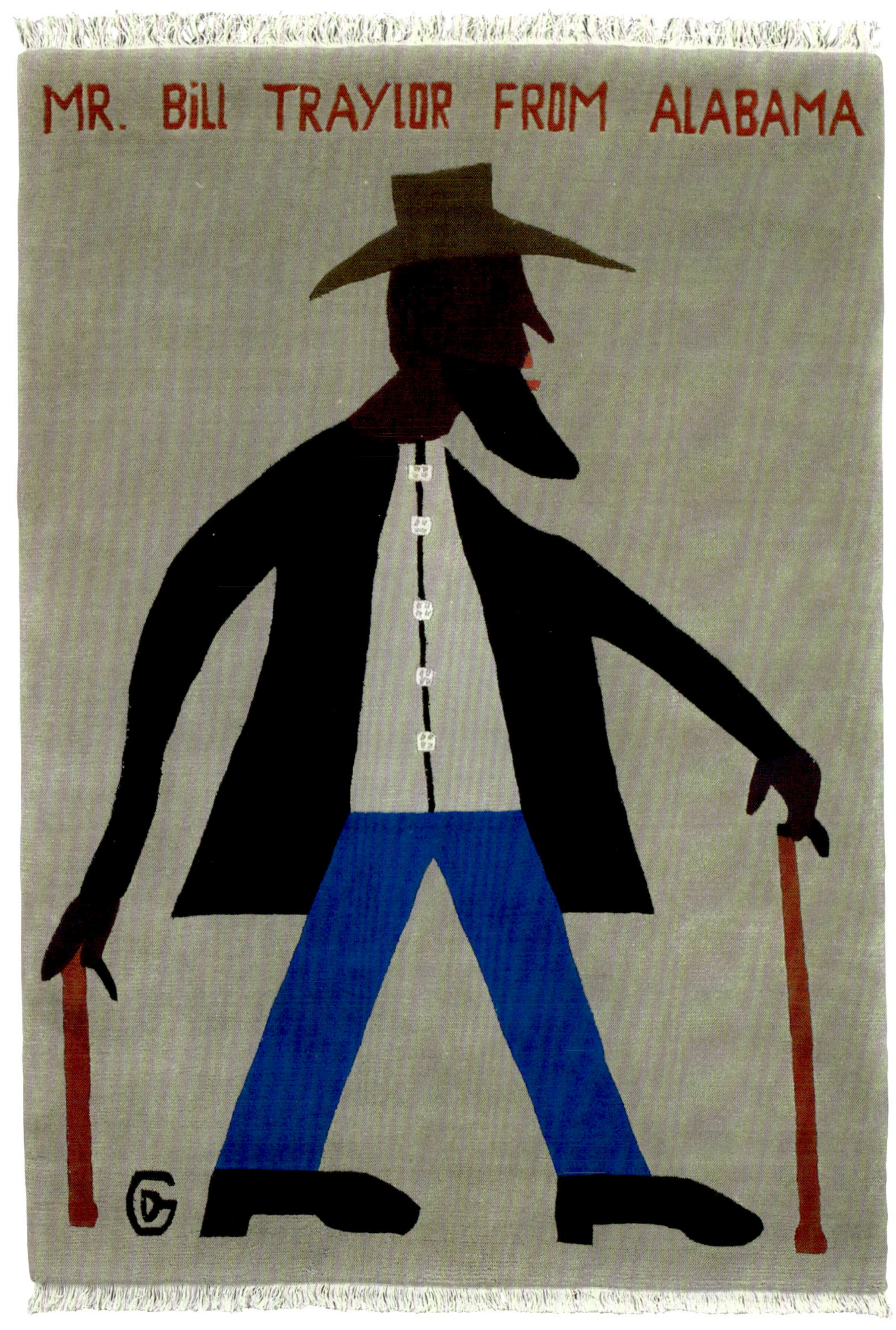

Mr. Bill Traylor, 1998

Bill Traylor's work has been a great source of inspiration to me. A self-taught artist, Traylor was a freed slave who began to draw at age 85.

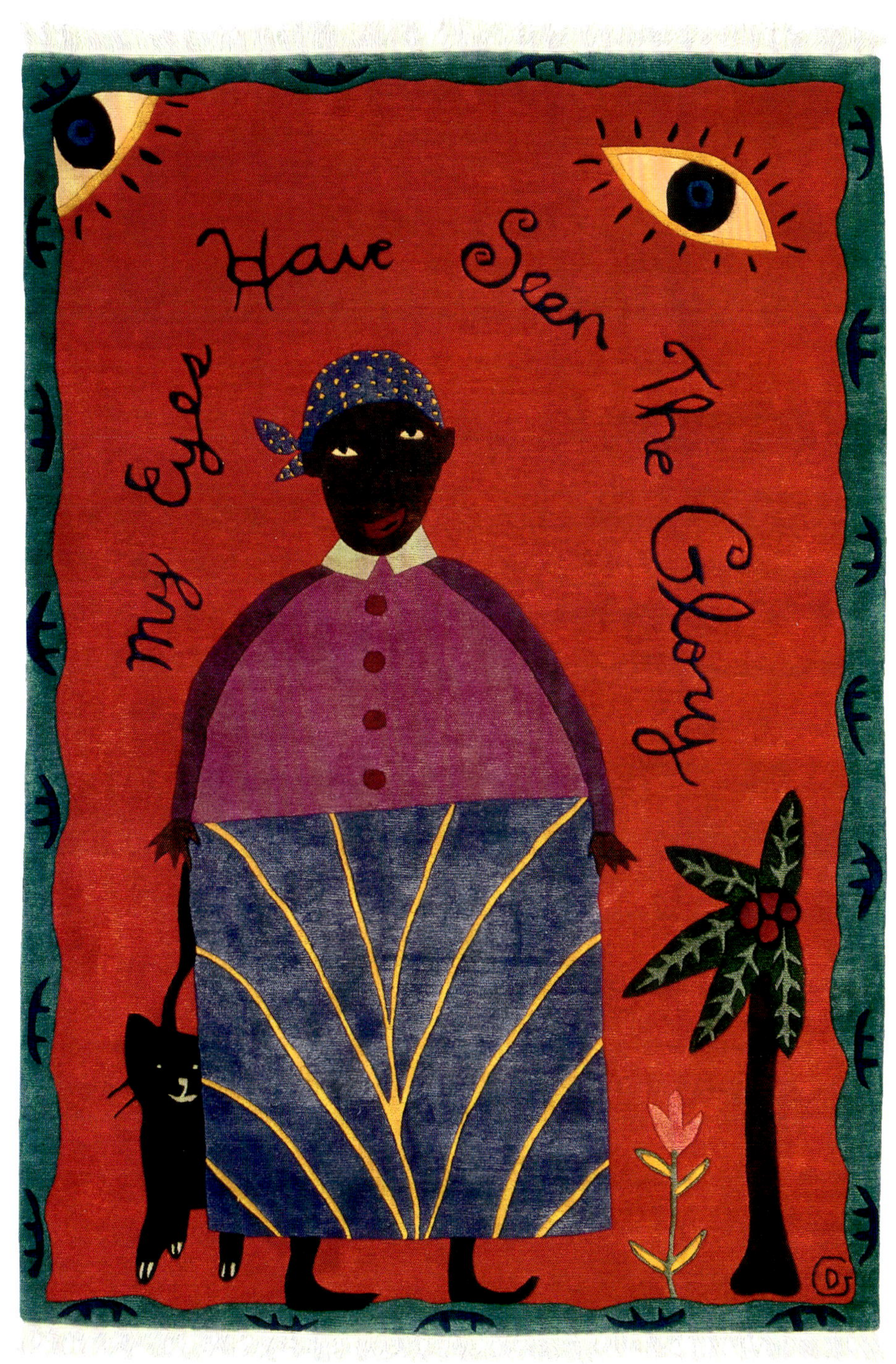

My Eyes Have Seen the Glory, 1995

Slavery was one of the saddest, most disgraceful atrocities in American history, along with the slaughter of the Native American nations.

Strange Fruit, 1998

Lewis Allan, a Jewish man, wrote the song "Strange Fruit," which Billie Holiday made famous. The lyrics graphically and hauntingly describe Ku Klux Klan lynchings, which still exist today.

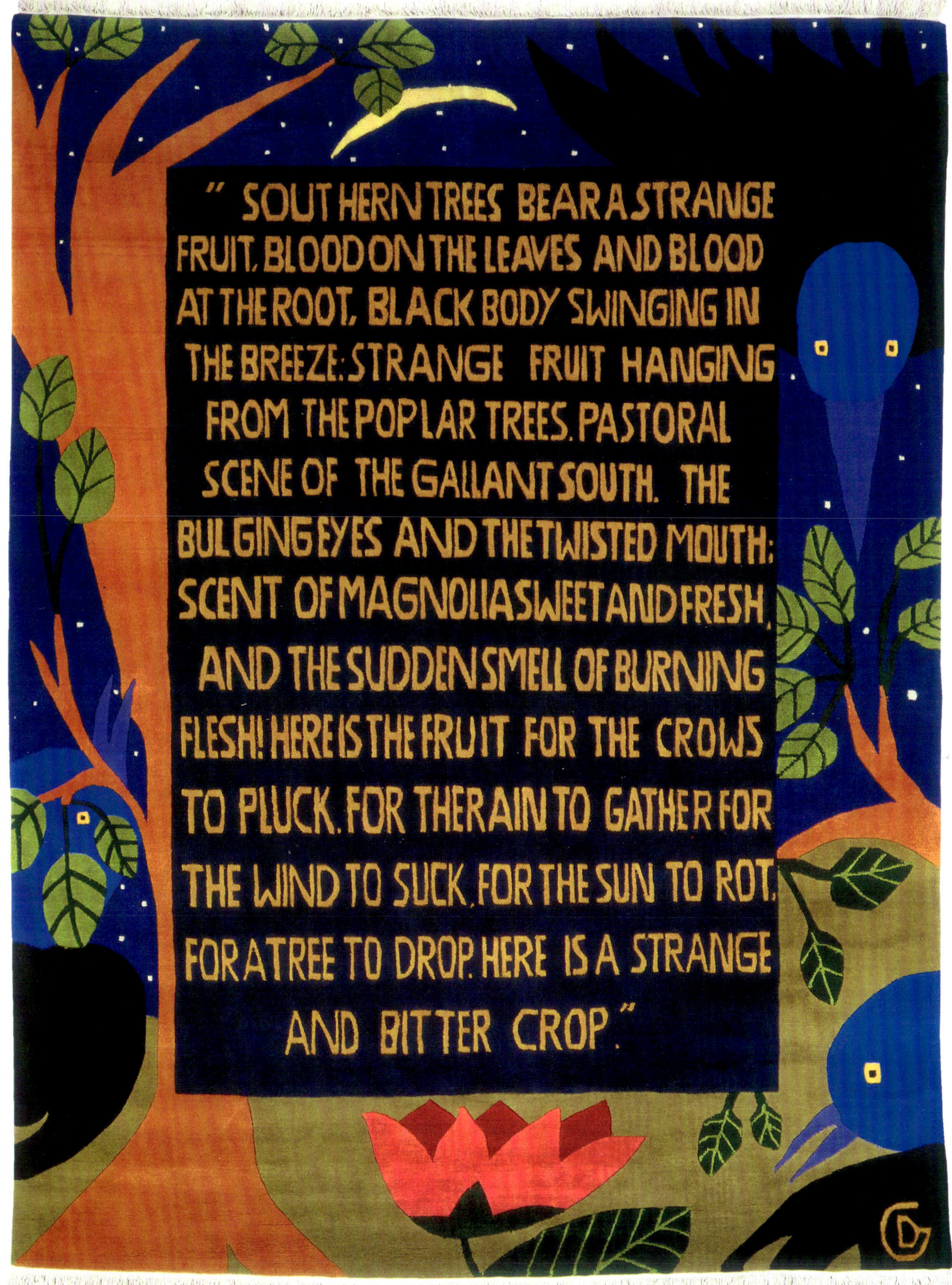
" SOUTHERN TREES BEAR A STRANGE
FRUIT, BLOOD ON THE LEAVES AND BLOOD
AT THE ROOT, BLACK BODY SWINGING IN
THE BREEZE: STRANGE FRUIT HANGING
FROM THE POPLAR TREES. PASTORAL
SCENE OF THE GALLANT SOUTH. THE
BULGING EYES AND THE TWISTED MOUTH:
SCENT OF MAGNOLIA SWEET AND FRESH,
AND THE SUDDEN SMELL OF BURNING
FLESH! HERE IS THE FRUIT FOR THE CROWS
TO PLUCK. FOR THE RAIN TO GATHER FOR
THE WIND TO SUCK. FOR THE SUN TO ROT,
FOR A TREE TO DROP. HERE IS A STRANGE
AND BITTER CROP."

Happier Times, 2002

Part of the Happy Series.

After September 11, 2001, I felt compelled to re-create our lost security, our lost loved ones, and our faith in the future.

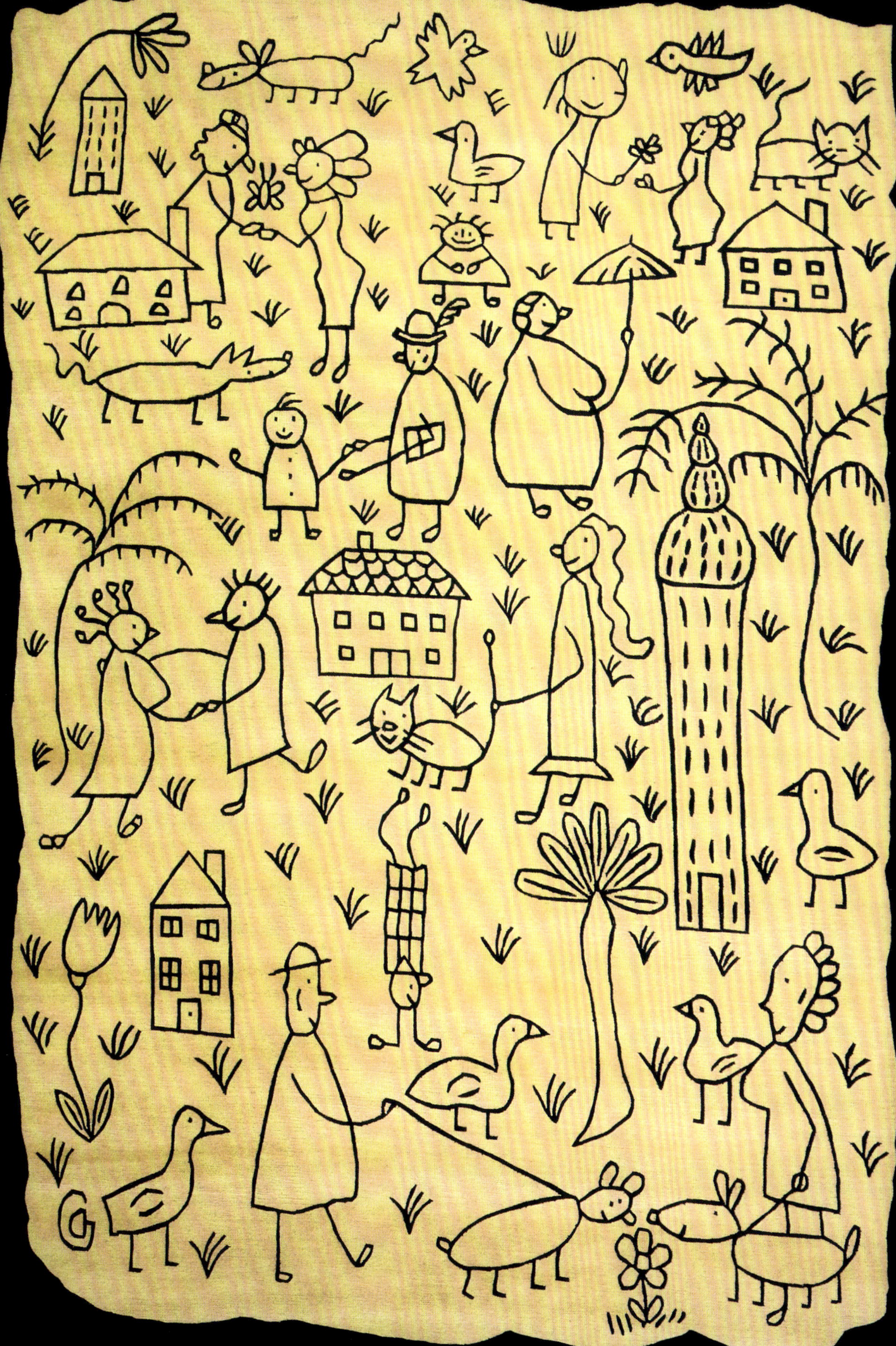

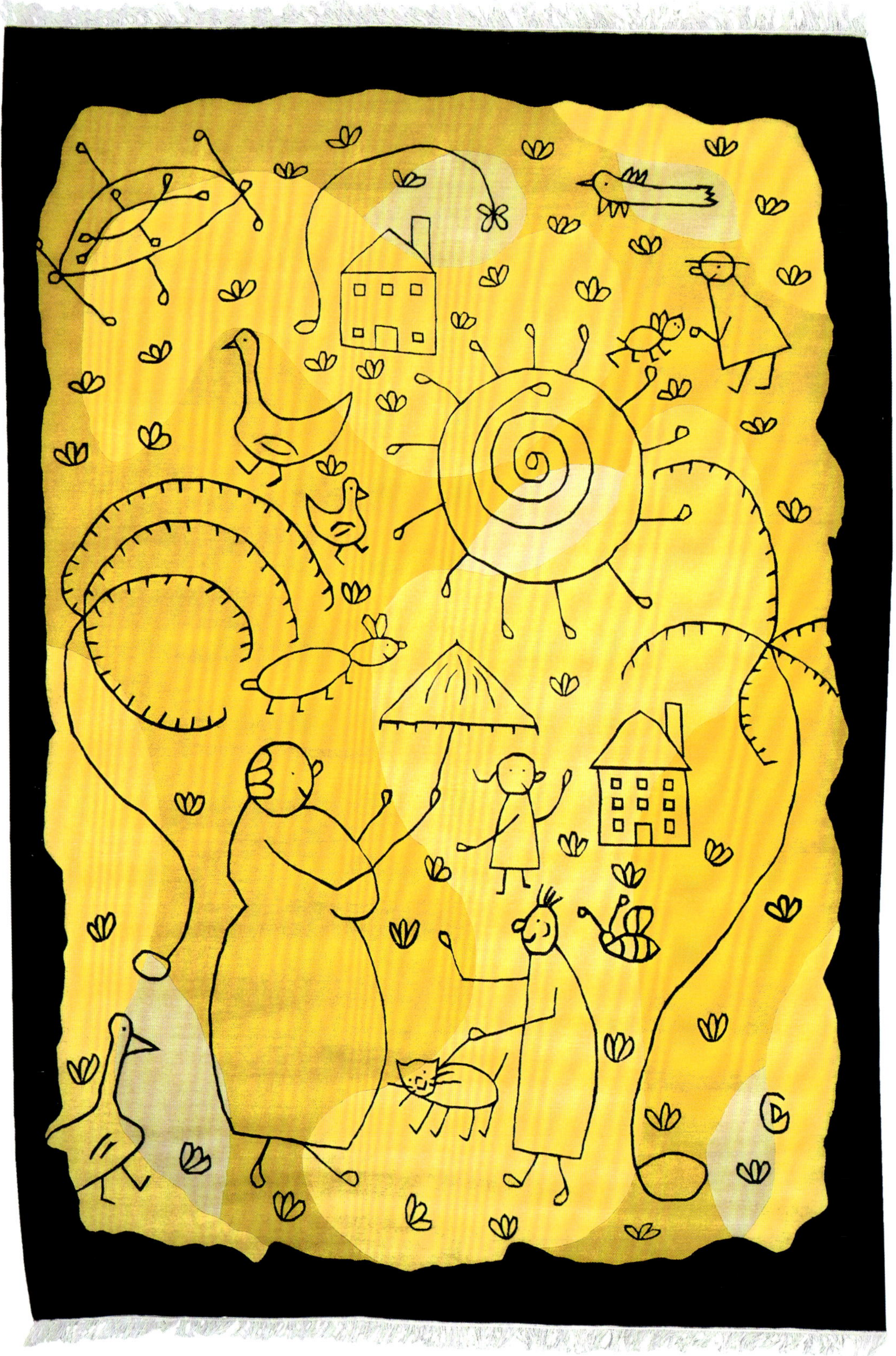

Happy Times, 2002

Part of the Happy Series.

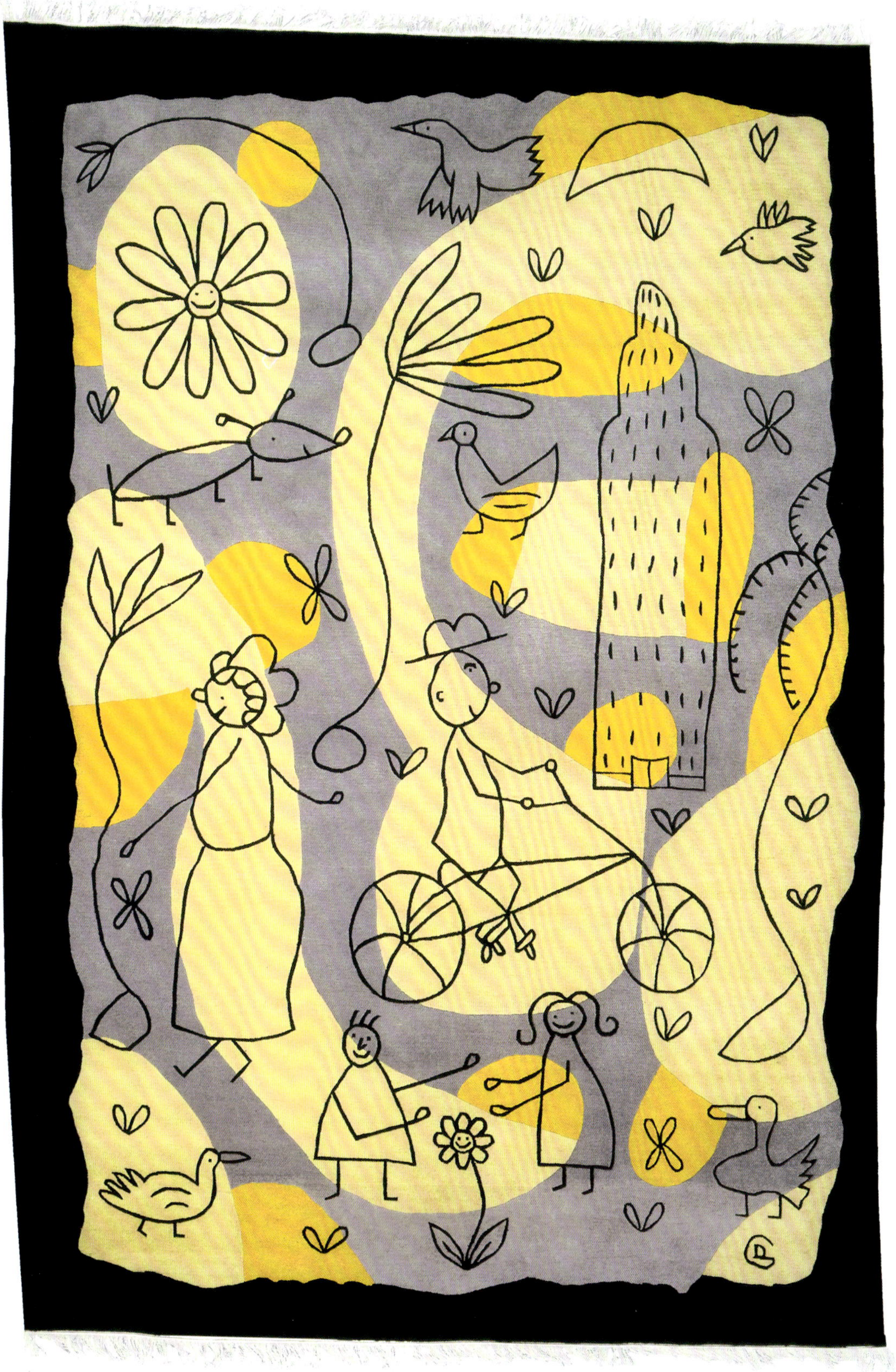

More Happy Times, 2002

Part of the Happy Series.

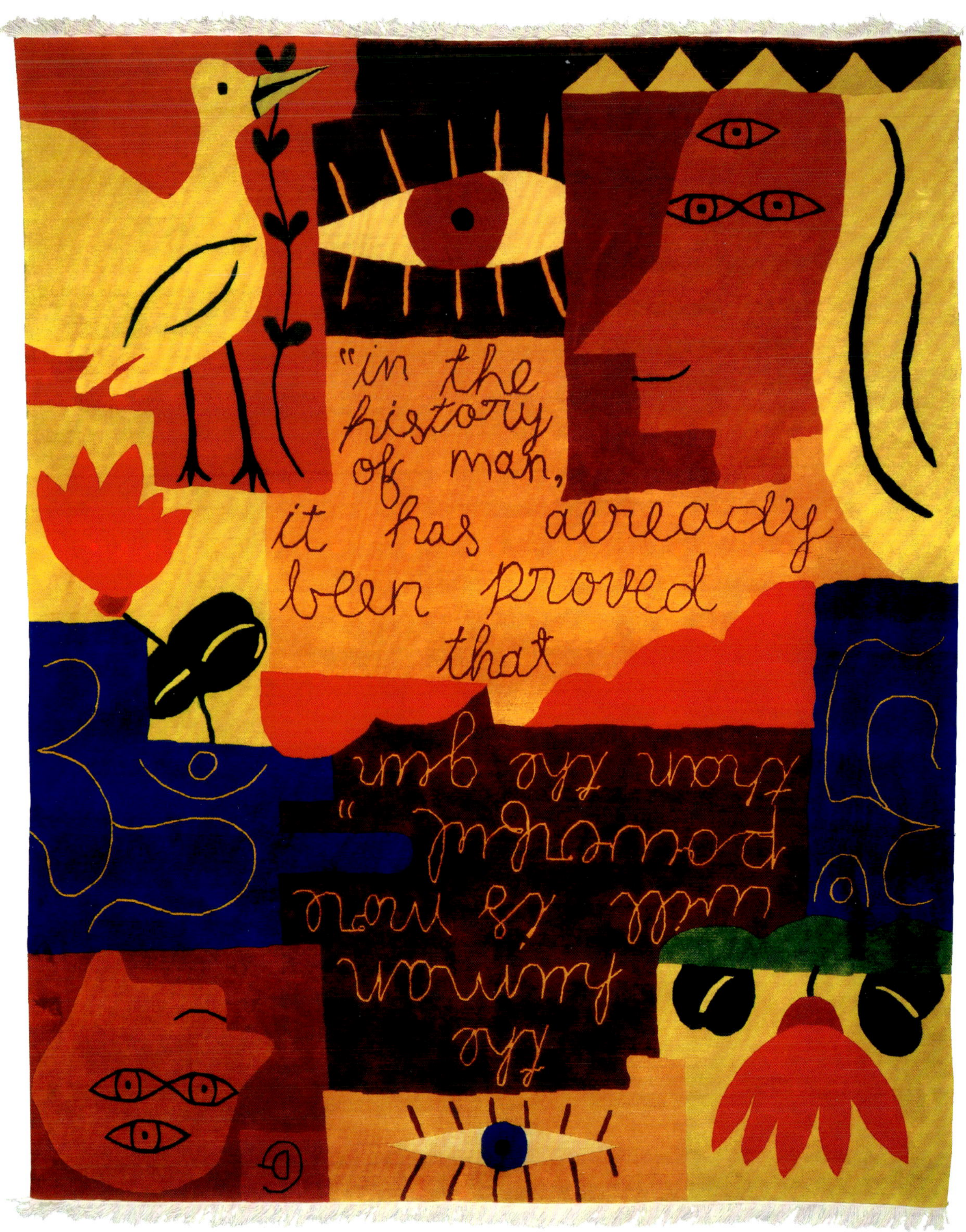

His Holiness the Dalai Lama, 2003

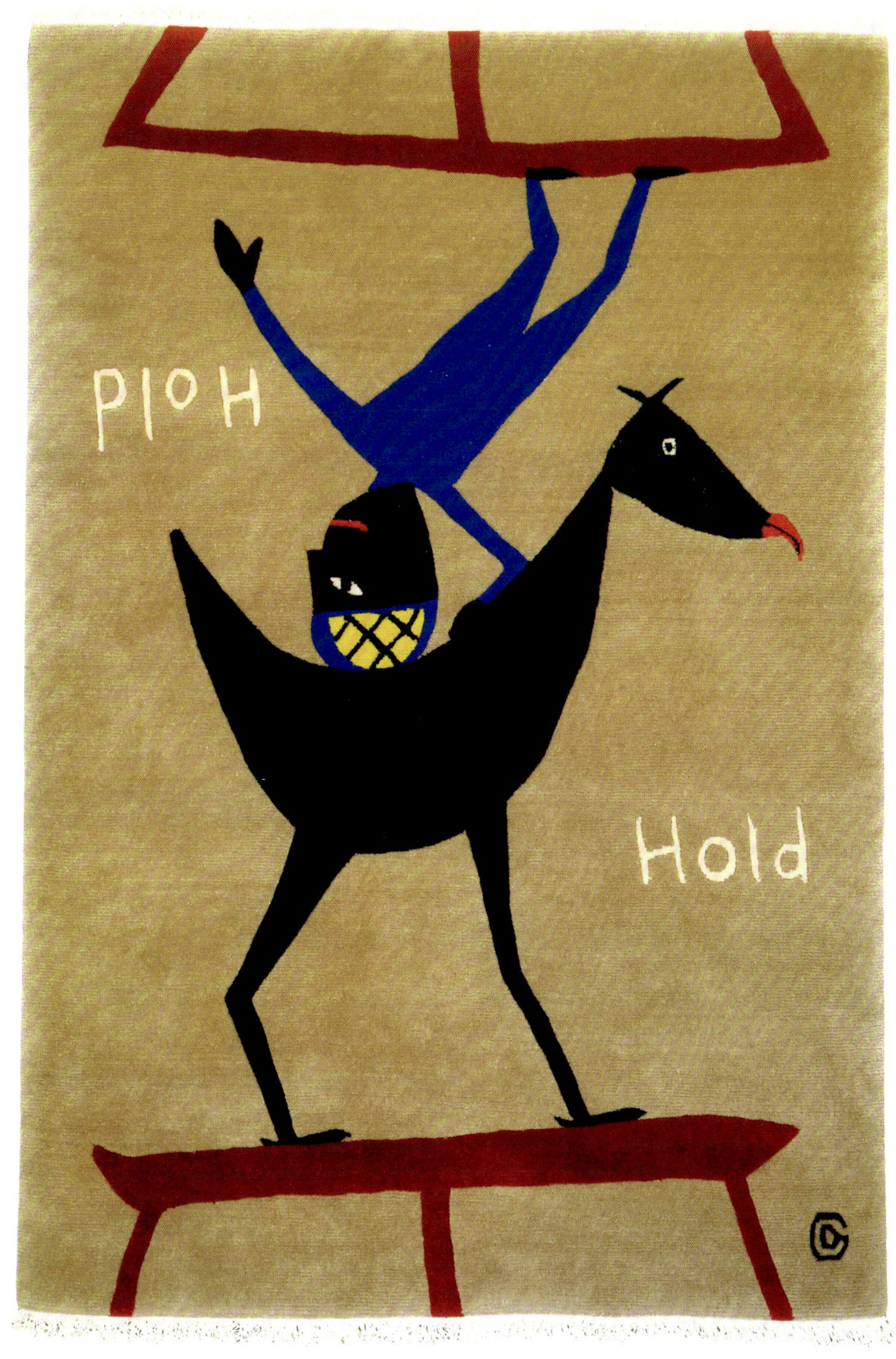

Hold, 1998

Inspired by Bill Traylor's work. Balance and trust accomplish great feats.

Shylock, 1998

Shakespeare's plea for equality, as spoken by Shylock in The Merchant of Venice. *This play has always been controversial. I chose to quote this portion of the soliloquy because the issue of anti-Semitism has never been addressed so beautifully before or since.*

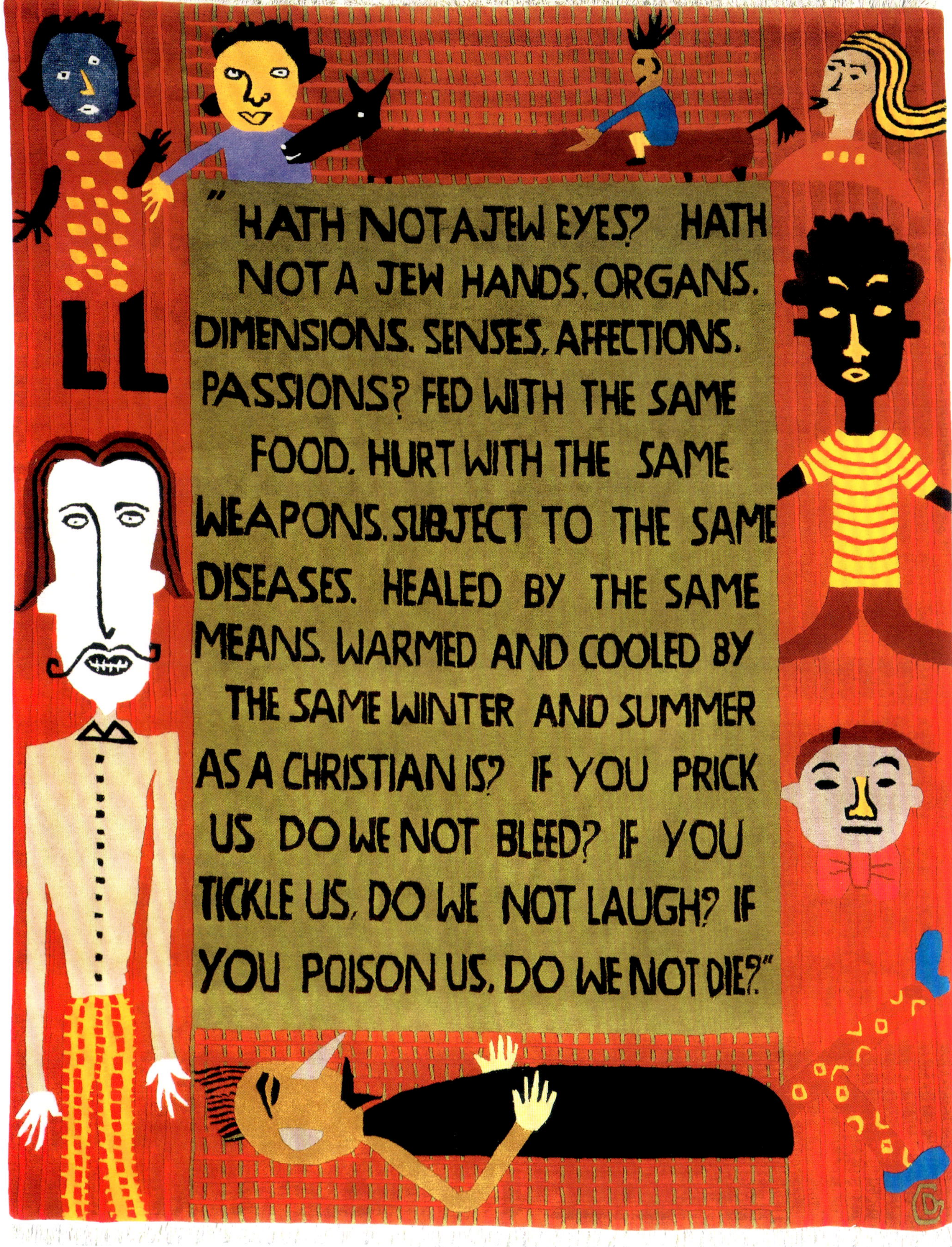
"HATH NOT A JEW EYES? HATH
NOT A JEW HANDS, ORGANS,
DIMENSIONS, SENSES, AFFECTIONS,
PASSIONS? FED WITH THE SAME
FOOD, HURT WITH THE SAME
WEAPONS, SUBJECT TO THE SAME
DISEASES, HEALED BY THE SAME
MEANS, WARMED AND COOLED BY
THE SAME WINTER AND SUMMER
AS A CHRISTIAN IS? IF YOU PRICK
US DO WE NOT BLEED? IF YOU
TICKLE US, DO WE NOT LAUGH? IF
YOU POISON US, DO WE NOT DIE?"

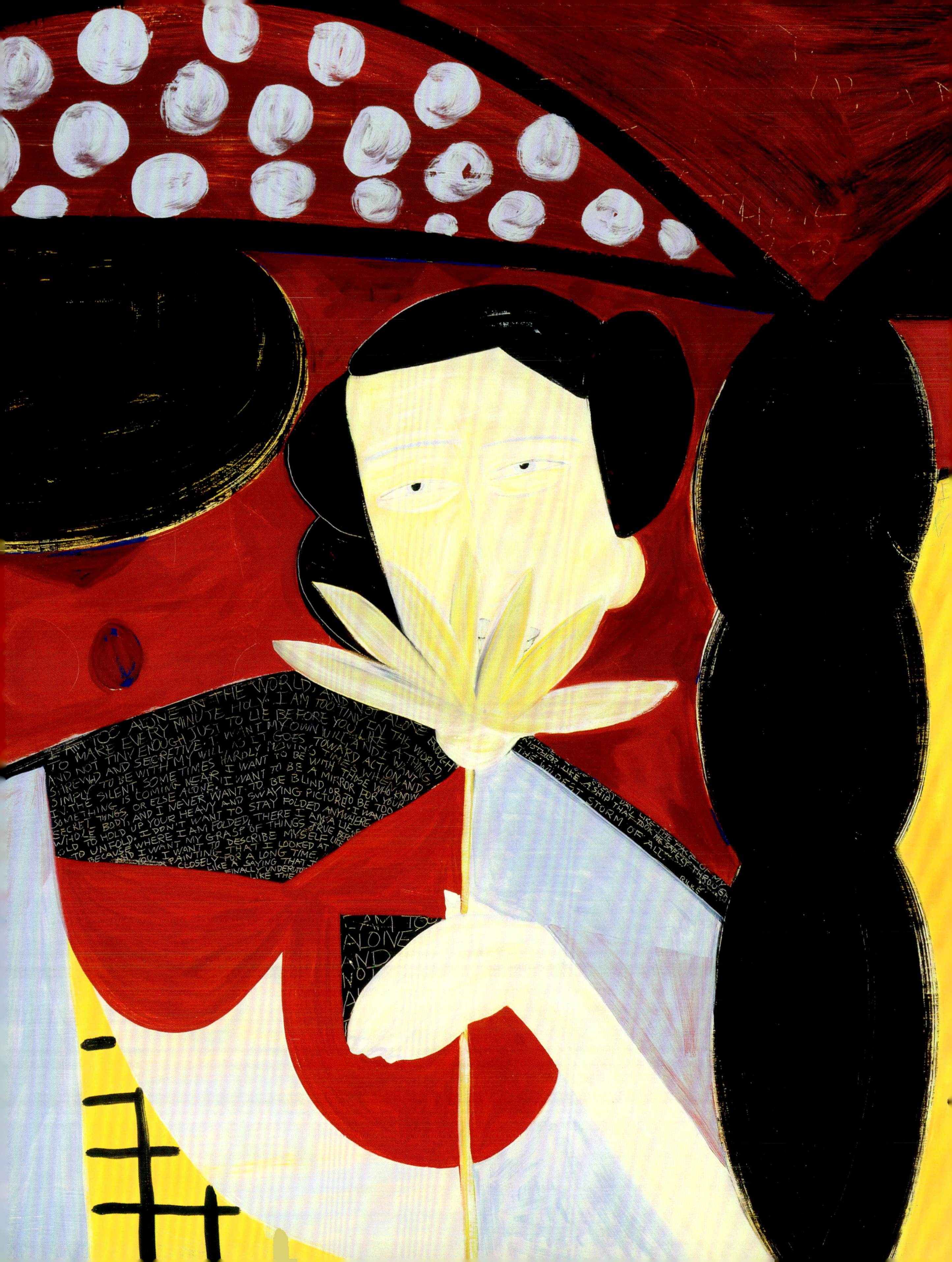
I AM TOO ALONE IN THE WORLD, AND NOT ALONE ENOUGH
TO MAKE EVERY MINUTE HOLY. I AM TOO TINY IN THIS WORLD,
AND NOT TINY ENOUGH JUST TO LIE BEFORE YOU LIKE A THING,
SHREWD AND SECRETIVE. I WANT MY OWN WILL, AND I WANT
SIMPLY TO BE WITH MY WILL AS IT GOES TOWARD ACTION, AND
IN THE SILENT, SOMETIMES HARDLY MOVING TIMES WHEN
SOMETHING IS COMING NEAR, I WANT TO BE WITH THOSE WHO KNOW
SECRET THINGS OR ELSE ALONE. I WANT TO BE A MIRROR FOR YOUR
WHOLE BODY, AND I NEVER WANT TO BE BLIND, OR TO BE TOO
OLD TO HOLD UP YOUR HEAVY AND SWAYING PICTURE. I WANT
TO UNFOLD. I DON'T WANT TO STAY FOLDED ANYWHERE,
BECAUSE WHERE I AM FOLDED, THERE I AM A LIE.
AND I WANT MY GRASP OF THINGS TRUE BEFORE
YOU. I WANT TO DESCRIBE MYSELF LIKE
A PAINTING THAT I LOOKED AT
CLOSELY FOR A LONG TIME,
LIKE A SAYING THAT I
FINALLY UNDERSTOOD,
LIKE THE
EVERY DAY, LIKE THE FACE OF MY
MOTHER, LIKE A SHIP THAT TOOK ME SAFELY THROUGH
THE WILDEST STORM OF ALL.
RILKE
I AM TOO
ALONE

paintings

The twelve paintings included in this exhibition reflect the emotional turmoil of oppression and its antidote—freedom.

—Dale Gottlieb

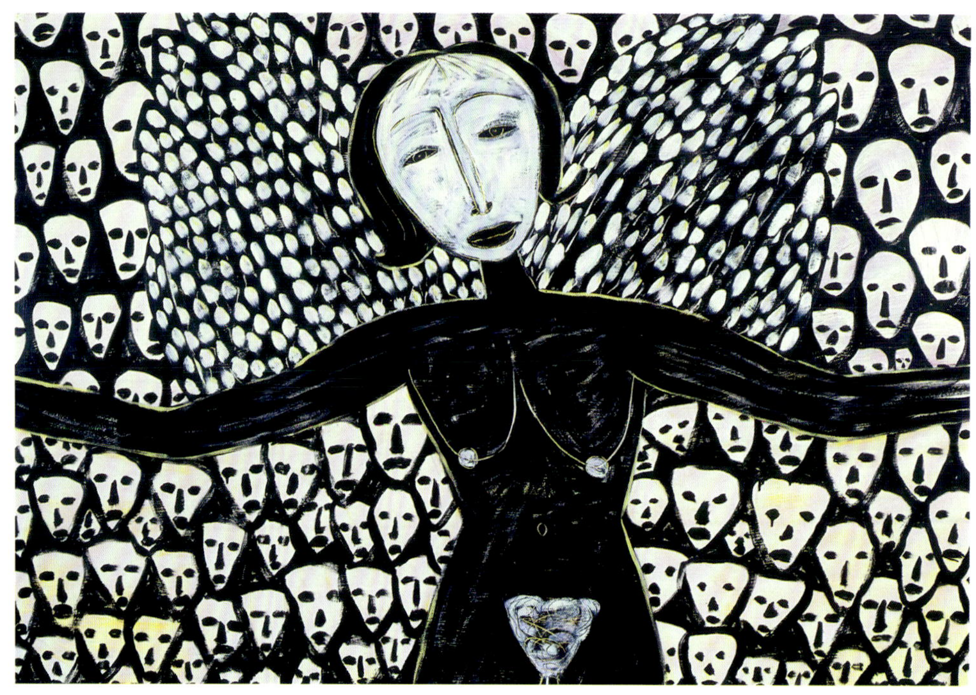

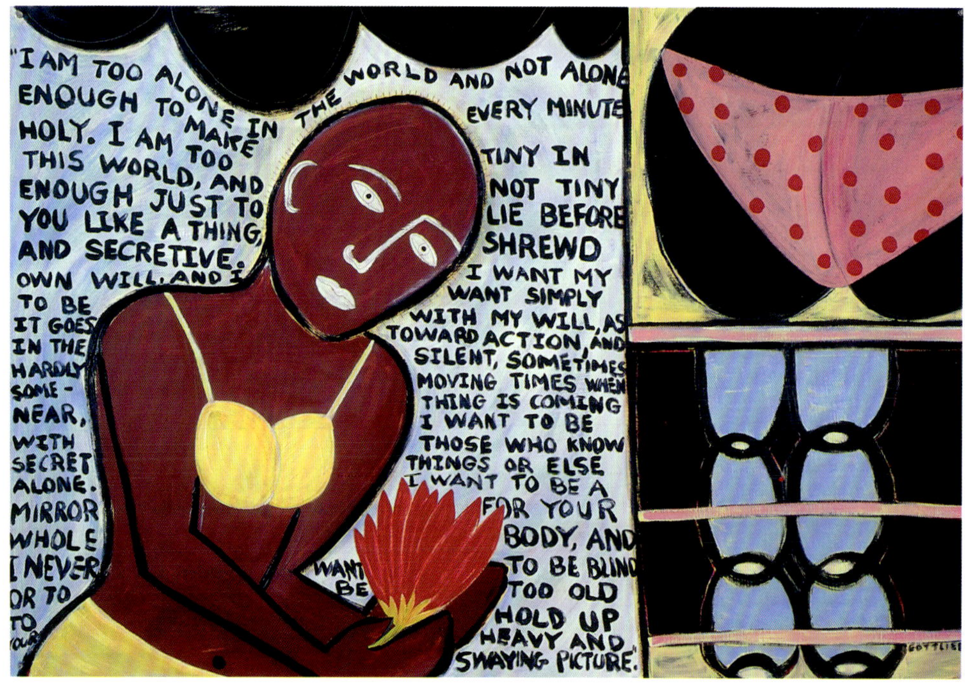

Philadelphia, 2001 *I Am Too Alone in the World and Not Alone Enough*, 2002

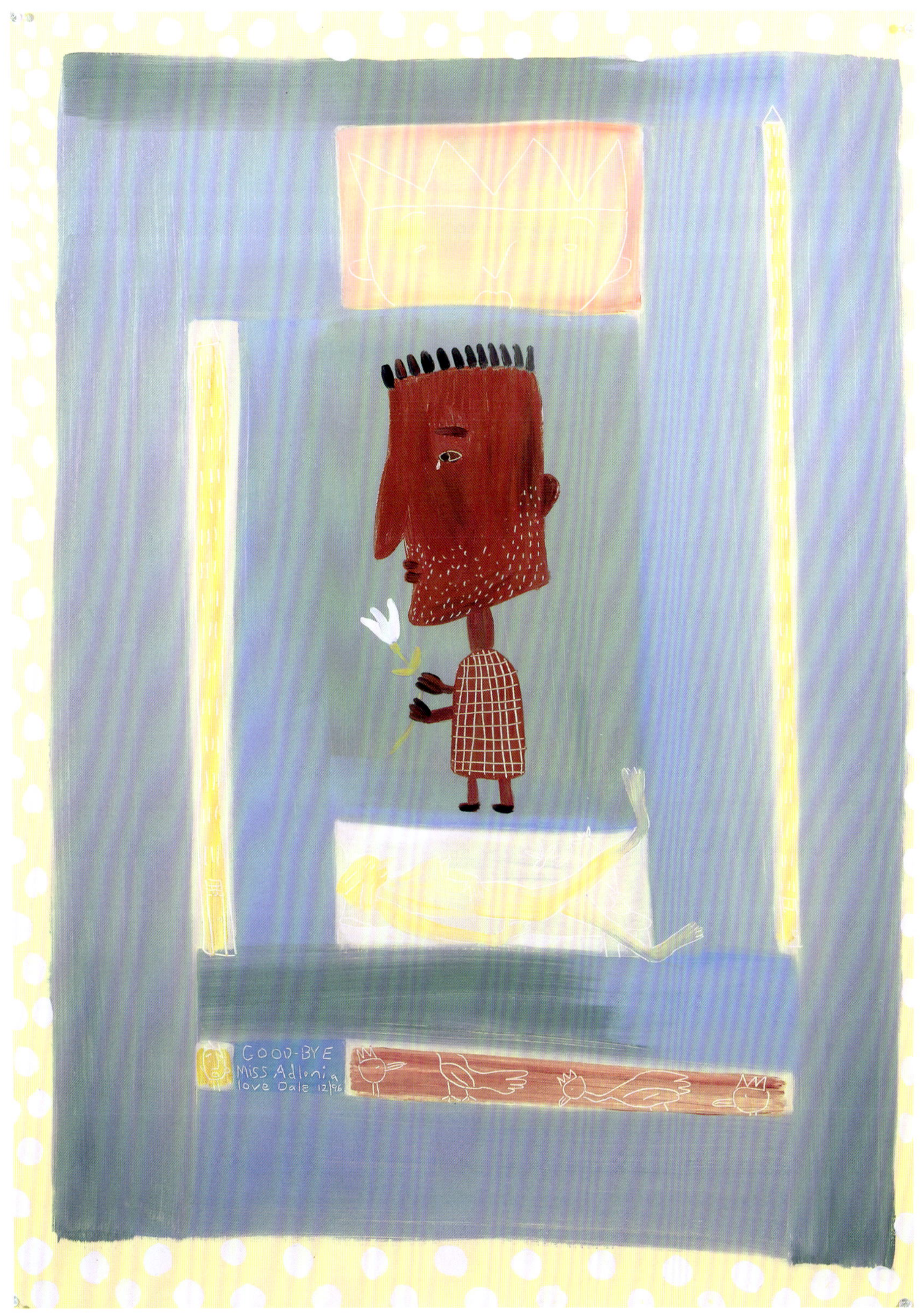

Goodbye Miss Adlonia, 1997

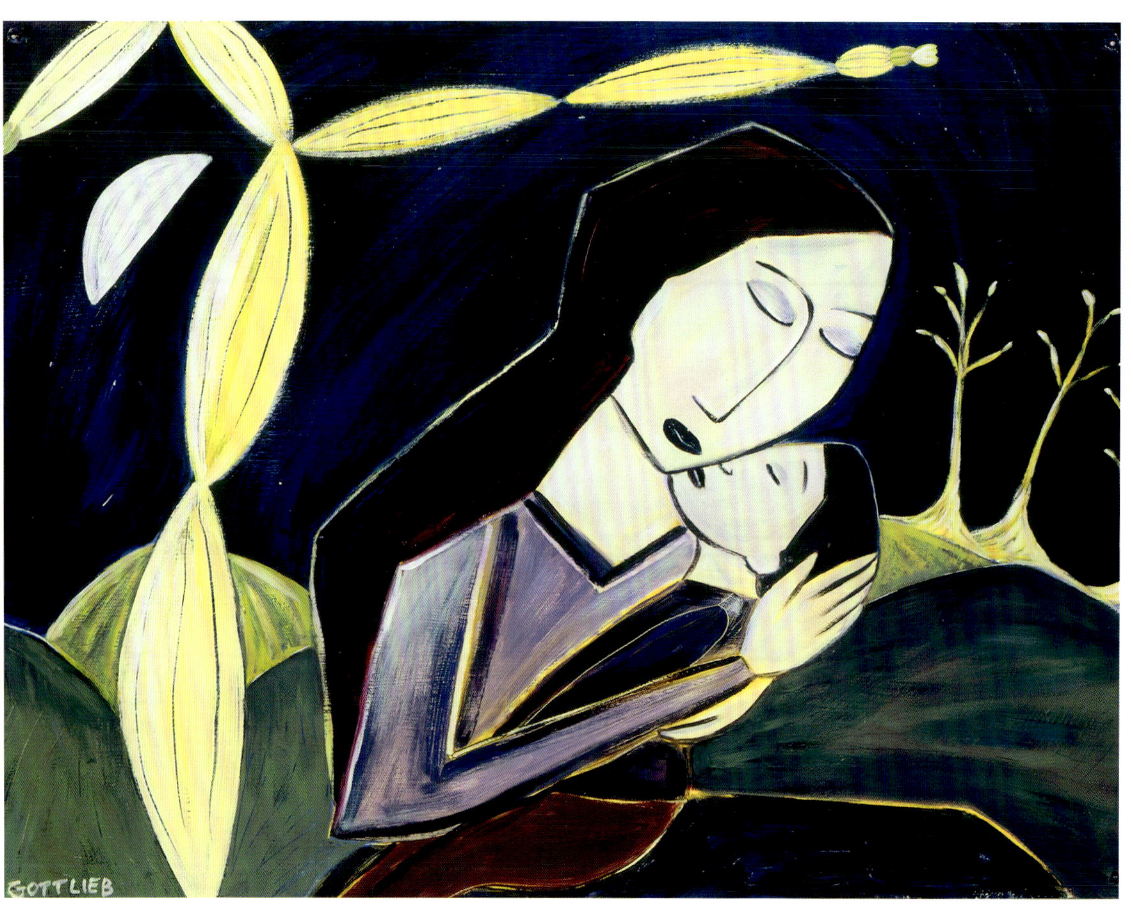

 Gathering Strength, 2000

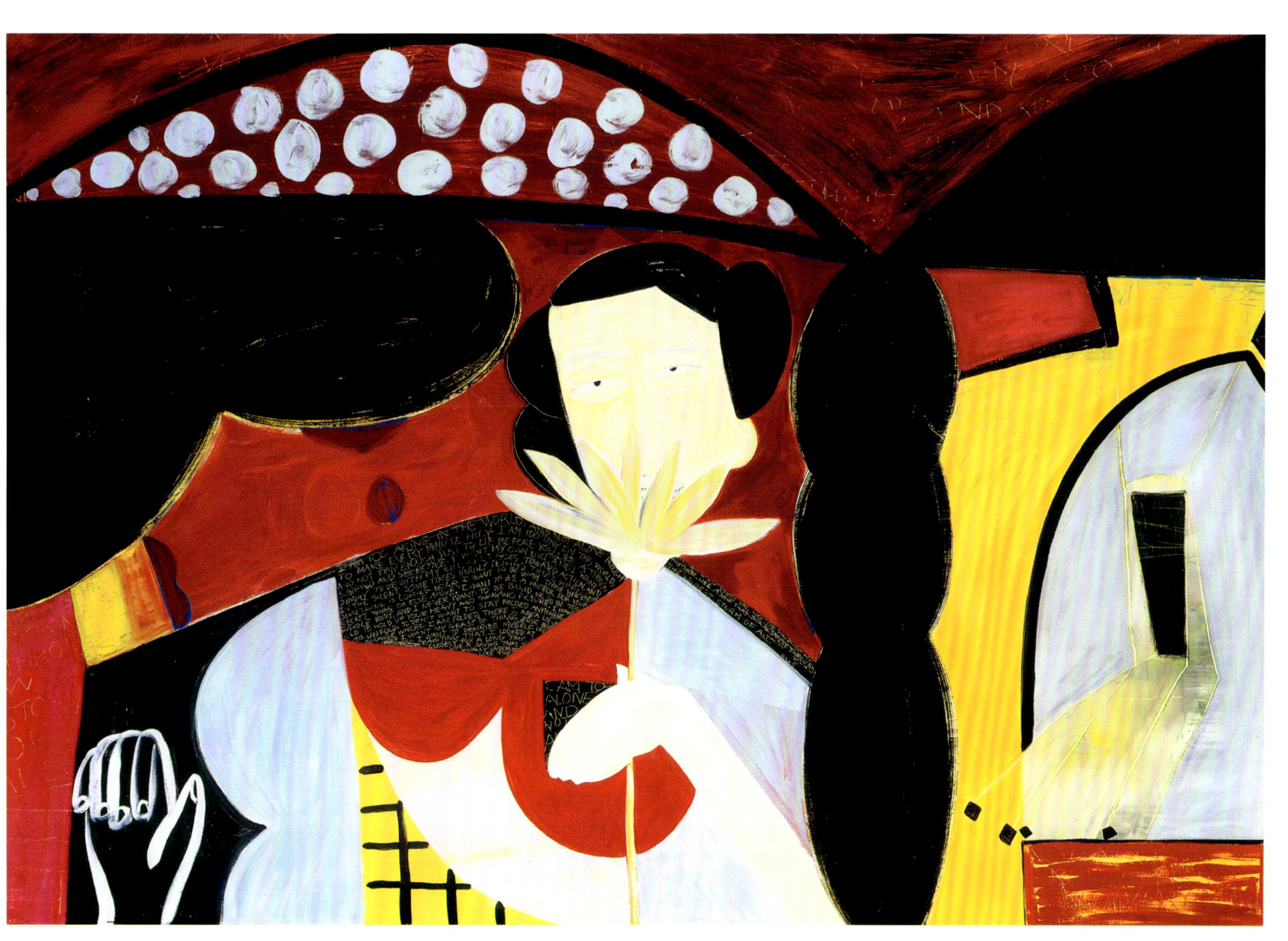

Rilke, 2001

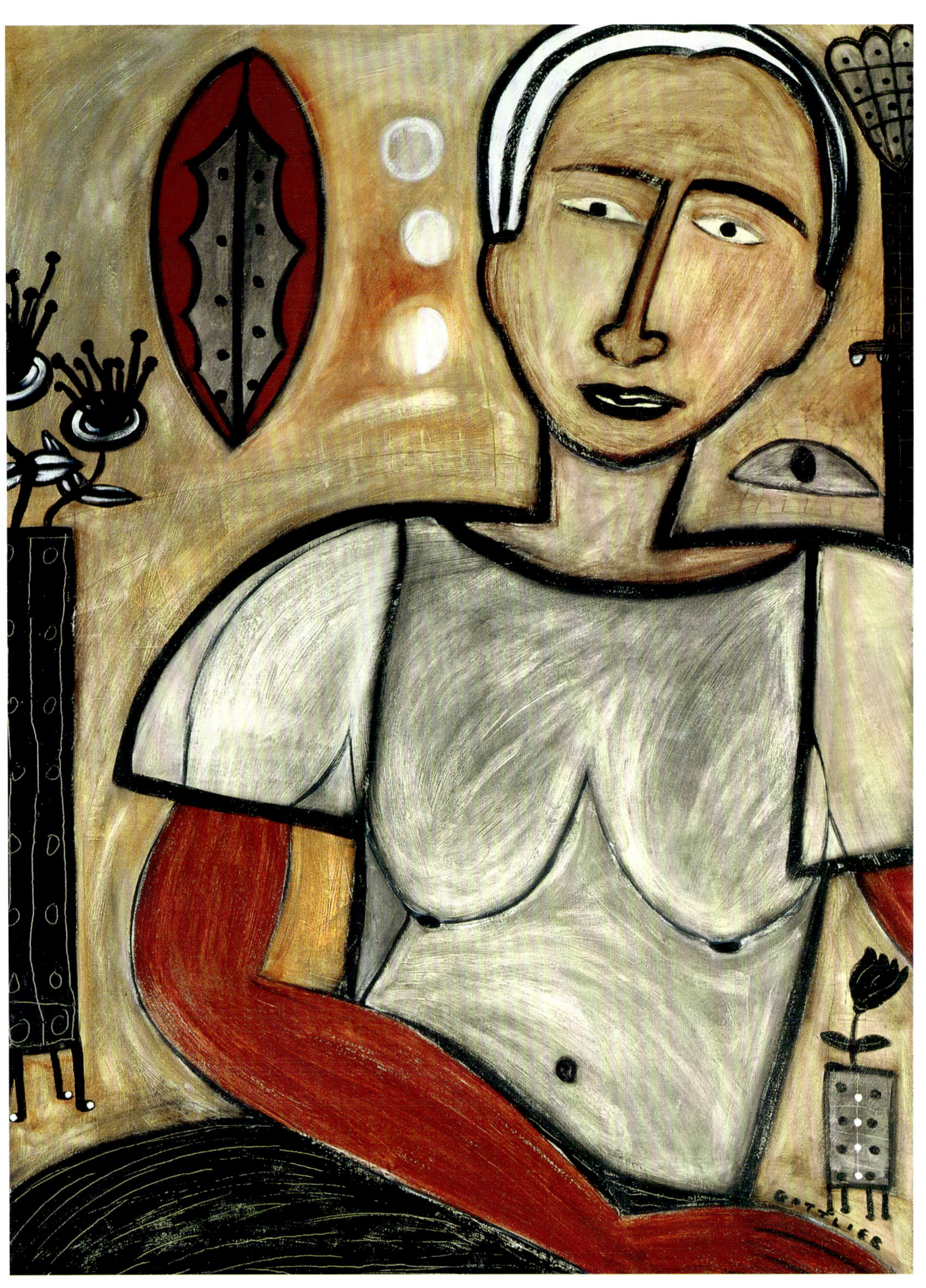

Neesey, 2002

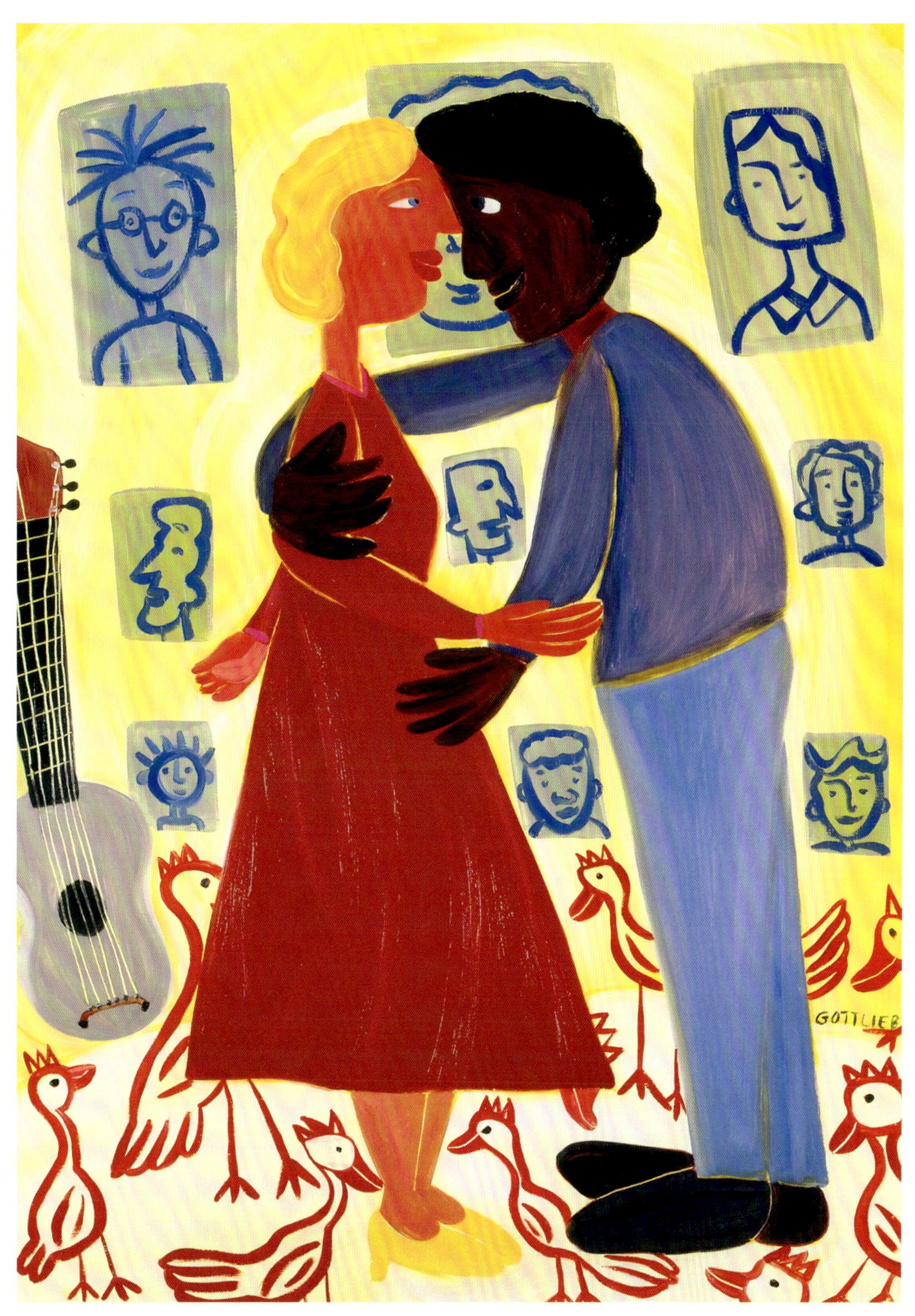

Chicken, 1997

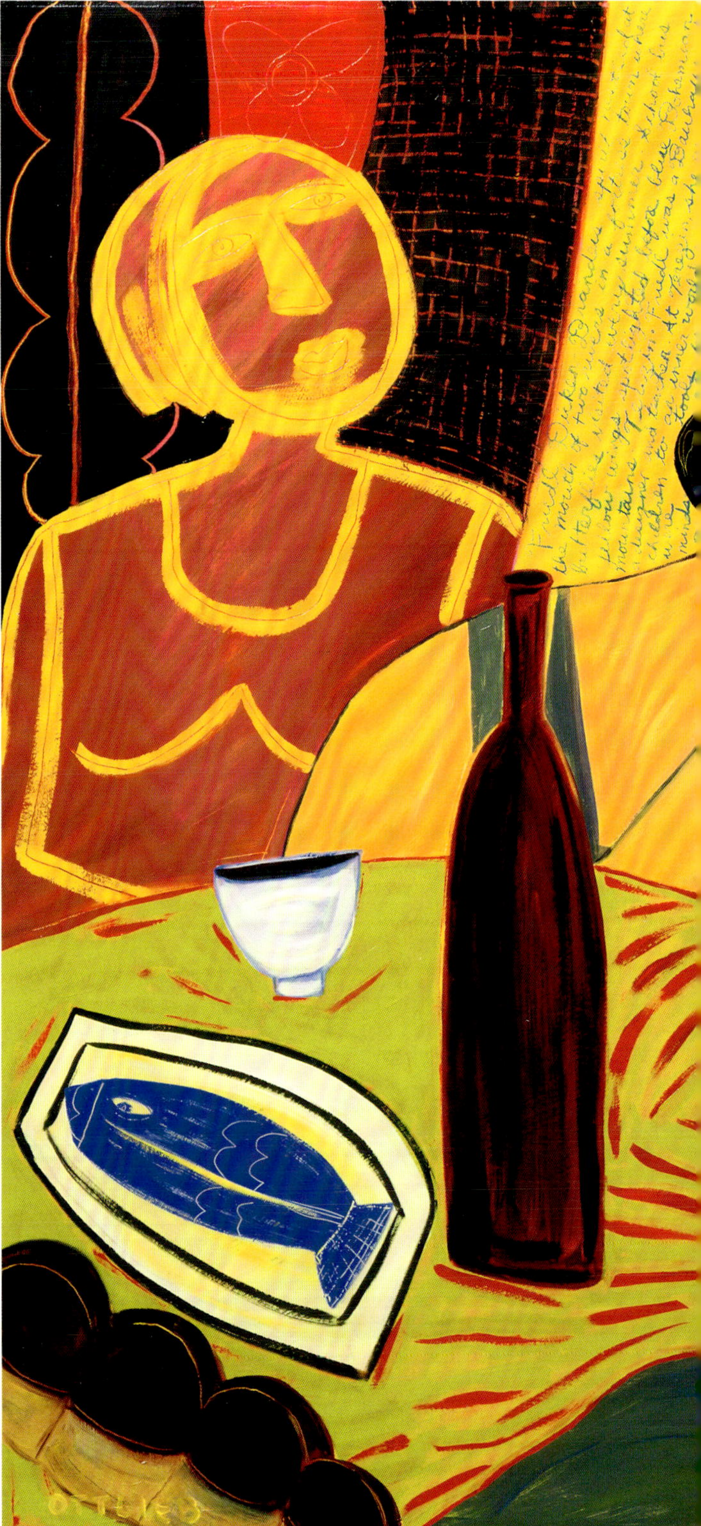

Friedle, 2000

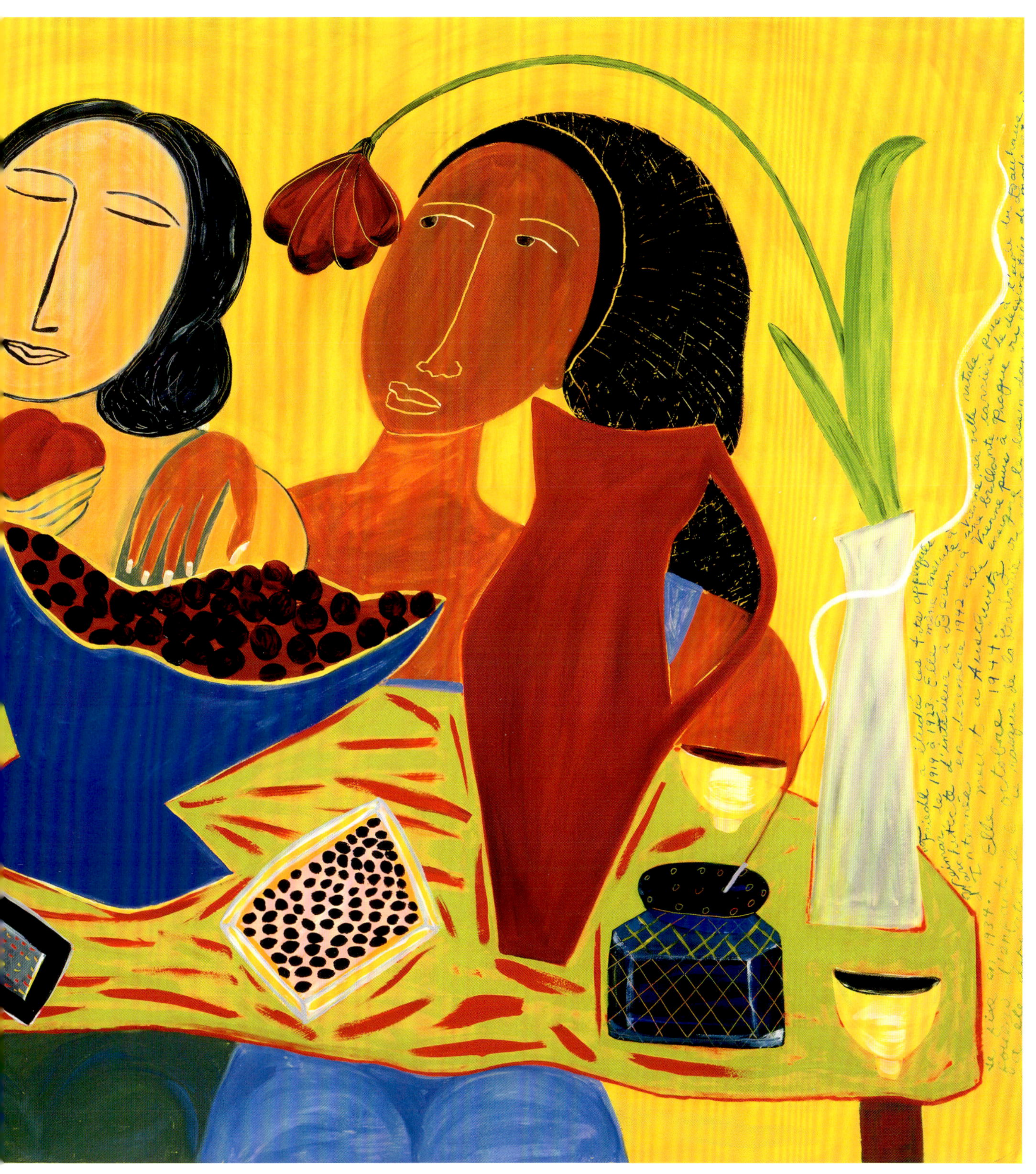

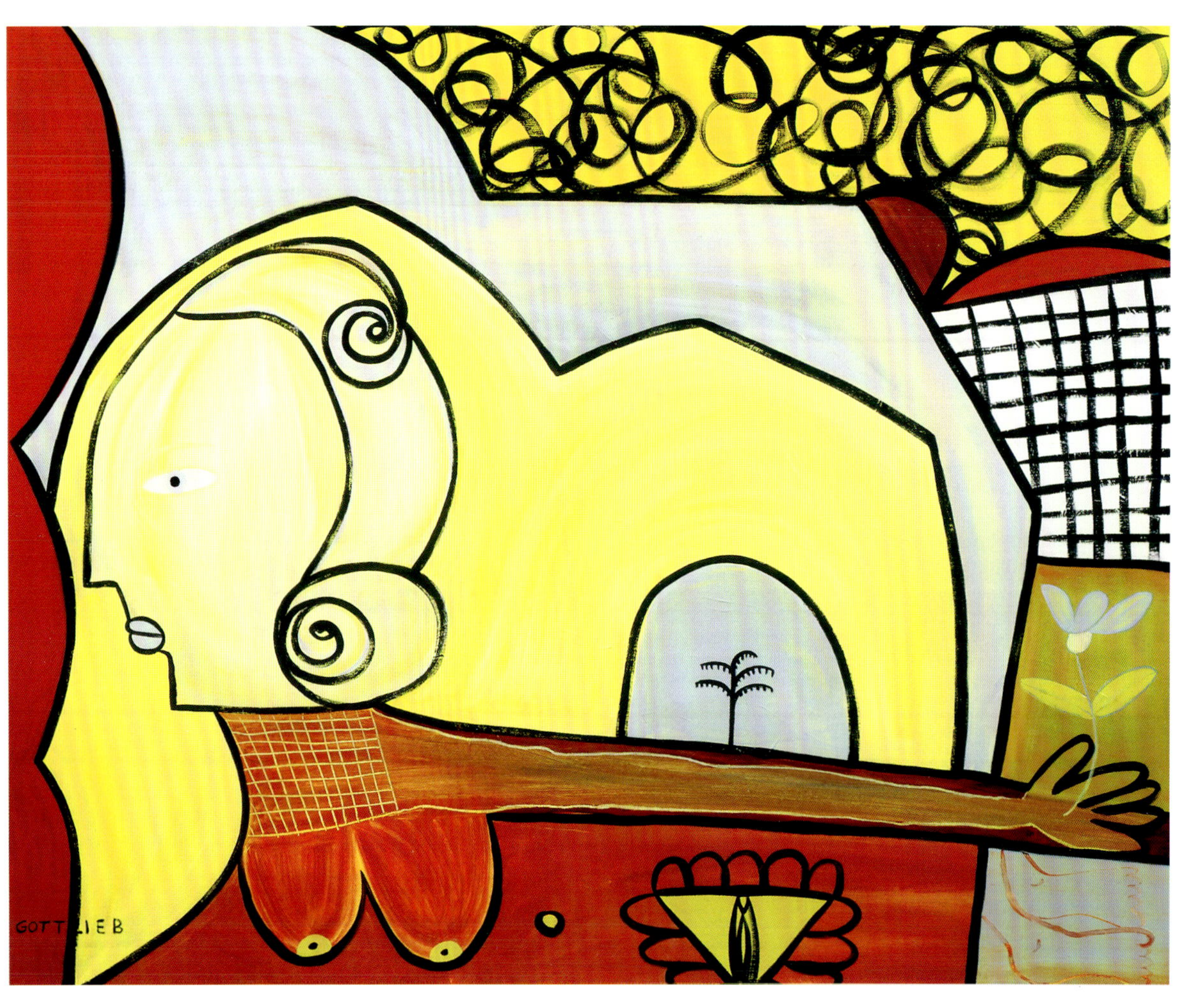

Survivor, 2000

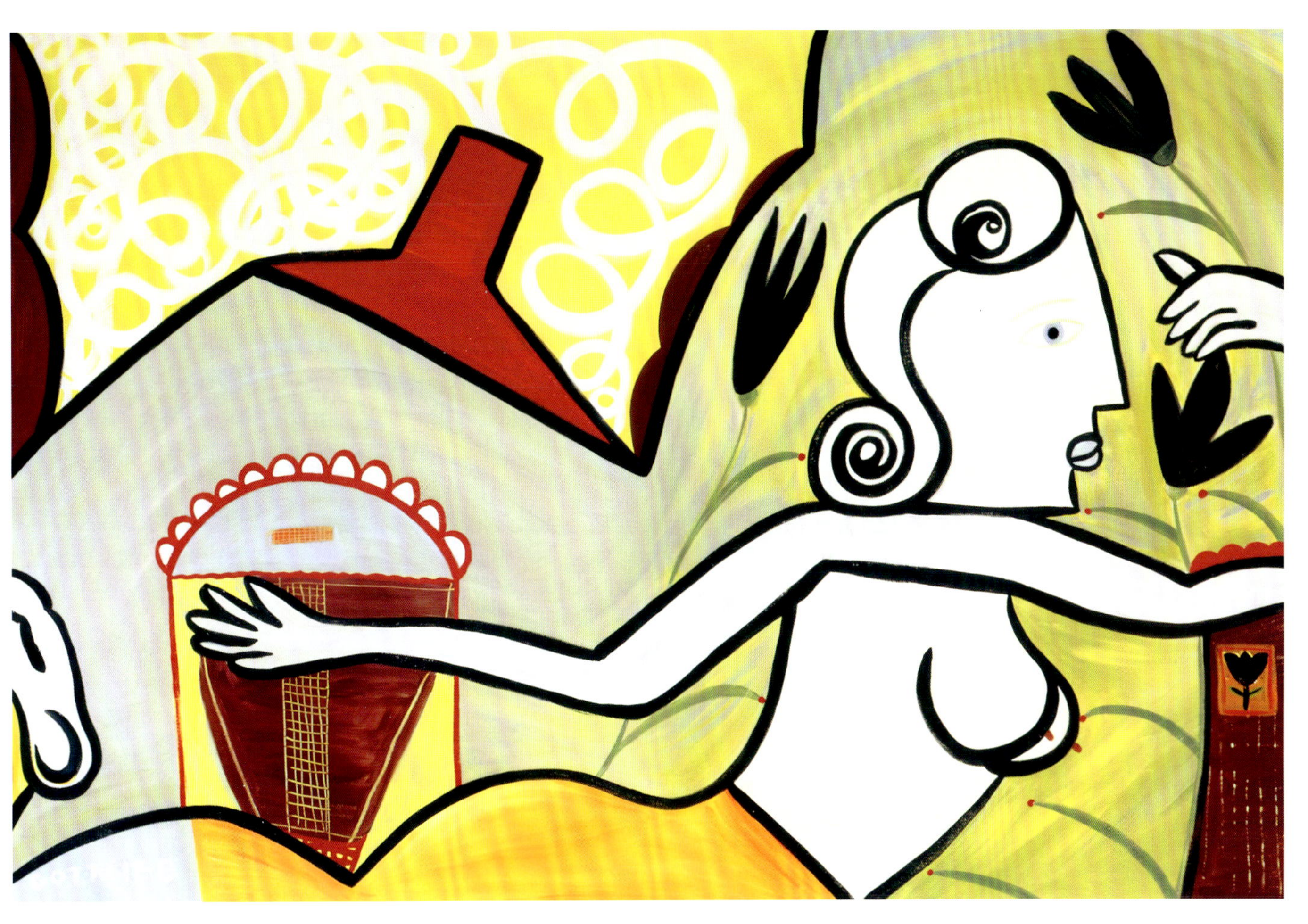

Free Moment, 2000

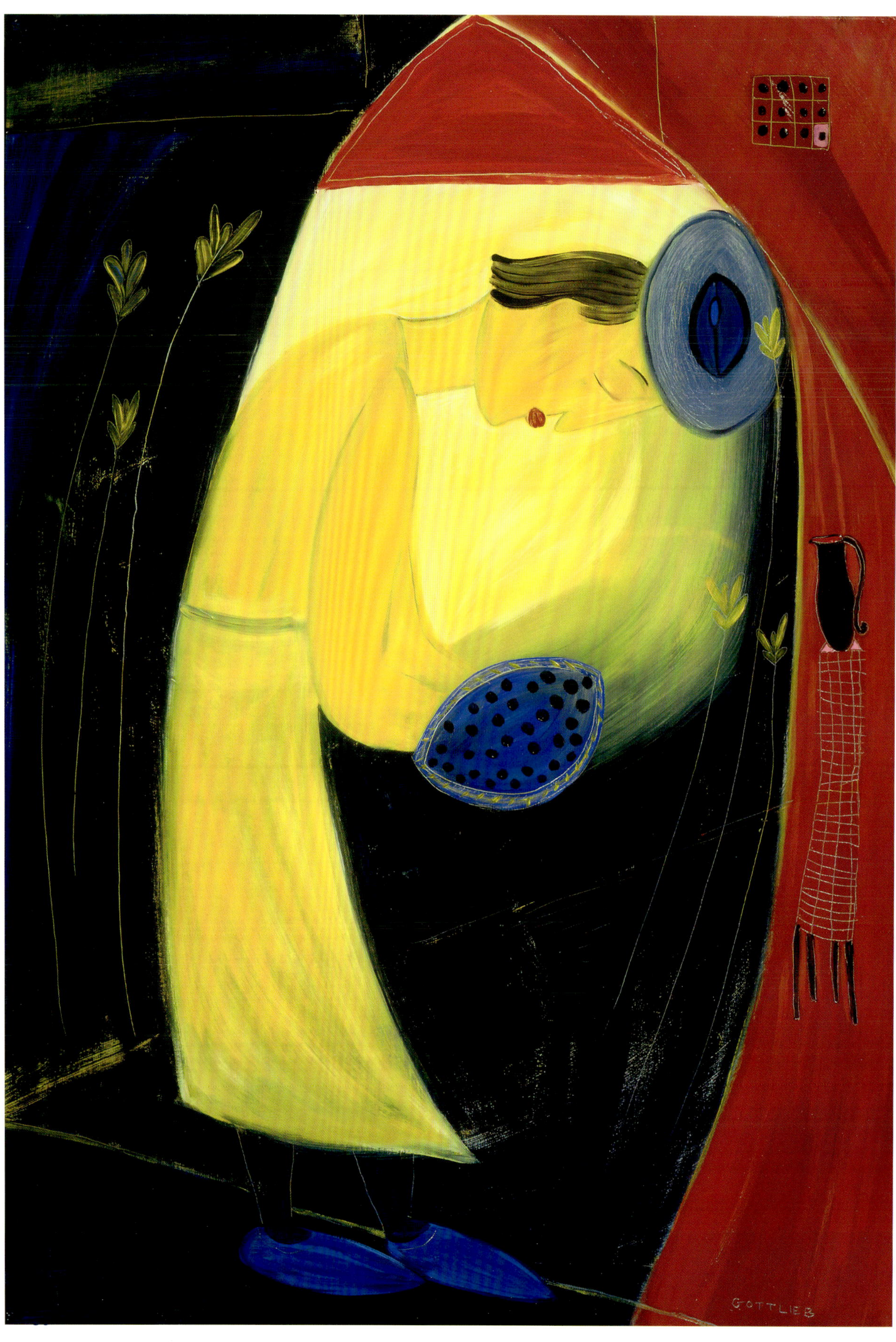
GOTTLIEB

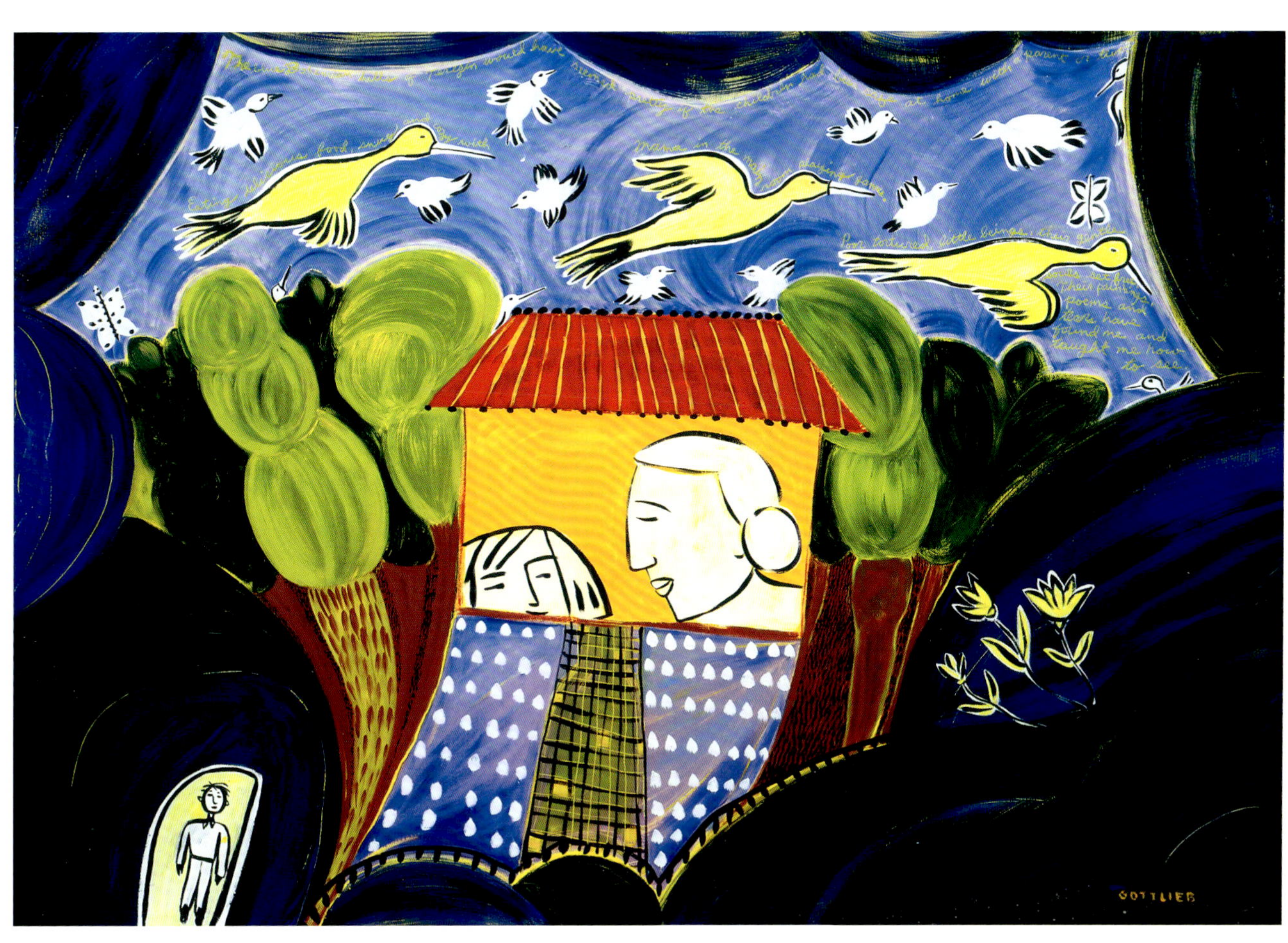

Gifted I, 1999 *Blue Bohemian Stage*, 2000

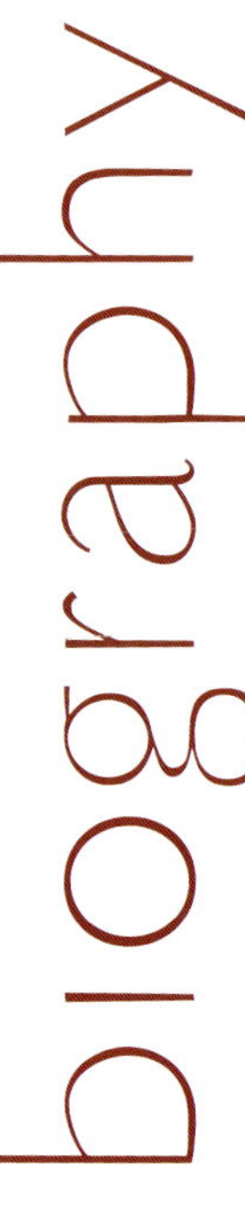

Dale Gottlieb

lives and works in Bellingham, Washington

Education

1975 BFA, School of Art and Design, Alfred University, Alfred, New York

Awards

1974 Levin's Award for outstanding undergraduate work

Solo Exhibitions

1981 City Hall, Claremont, New Hampshire
1985 Mink Brook Gallery, Hanover, New Hampshire
1991 Blue Horse Gallery, Bellingham
1992 Blue Horse Gallery, Bellingham
1994 MIA Gallery, Seattle
1996 Every Picture Tells a Story, Los Angeles
1996 Auburn City Hall, Auburn, Washington
1996 Mia Gallery, Seattle
1998 Davidson Gallery, Seattle
2000 Davidson Gallery, Seattle
2003 Lucia Douglas Gallery, Bellingham

Group Exhibitions

1981 Linde Tracey Gallery, Boston
1982 The Water Media Biennial, Zaner Gallery, Rochester, New Hampshire
1982 New Hampshire State House, Concord
1983 University of New Hampshire, Durham
1984 Society of Illustrators, New York
1985 Pleidas Gallery, New York
1986 *Myths and Magic*, Rye Art Center, Rye, New York
1987 Gallery 454 North, Los Angeles
1989 Lumina Gallery, San Francisco
1990 Blue Horse Gallery, Bellingham
1990 Every Picture Tells a Story, Los Angeles
1991 Society of Illustrators, New York
1992 Society of Illustrators, New York
1993 Society of Illustrators, New York
1993 *Tales and Traditions: Storytelling in 20th-Century American Craft*, Whatcom Museum of History & Art, Bellingham; curated by Lloyd Herman and Matthew Kangas
1995 Society for Contemporary Crafts, Pittsburgh
1995 *Art from Children's Books*, Bellevue Art Museum, Bellevue, Washington
1996 *Worlds of Wonder: Art of Children's Books*, Whatcom Museum of History & Art, Bellingham
1996 Gallery 500, Philadelphia
1998 Muse Image, Santa Fe, New Mexico
1999 Lucia Douglas Gallery, Bellingham

Artwork for Film

1987 *Surrender*, dir. Jerry Belson; designed the artwork for the struggling artist character played by Sally Field

Children's Books

Big Dog
written and illustrated by Dale Gottlieb
William and Morrow, 1989

An Alligator Lives in Benjamin's House
written by Nancy Van Caster and illustrated by Dale Gottlieb
Philomel, 1990

Are We There Yet?
written by Harriet Ziefert and illustrated by Dale Gottlieb
Bantam, 1990

My Stories by Hildy Calpurnia Rose
written and illustrated by Dale Gottlieb
Knopf, 1991

Seeing Eye Willie
written and illustrated by Dale Gottlieb
Knopf, 1992

Train Leaves the Station
written by Eve Mirriam and illustrated by Dale Gottlieb
Henry Holt, 1992

A Christmas Carol
written by Sara Teasdale and illustrated by Dale Gottlieb
Henry Holt, 1993

I Got a Family
written by Melrose Cooper and illustrated by Dale Gottlieb
Henry Holt, 1993

Taxi! Taxi!
written by Cari Best and illustrated by Dale Gottlieb
Little Brown, 1994

I Got Community
written by Melrose Cooper and illustrated by Dale Gottlieb
Henry Holt, 1995

Jackal's Flying Lesson
written by Verna Ardema and illustrated by Dale Gottlieb
Knopf, 1995

Watermelon Day
written by Kathi Appelt and illustrated by Dale Gottlieb
Henry Holt, 1996

Where Jamaica Go?
written and illustrated by Dale Gottlieb
Orchard Books, 1996

Bottom of the Ninth
written and illustrated by Dale Gottlieb
Kingfisher Books, 1997

Ms. Sneed's Guide to Hygiene
written and illustrated by Dale Gottlieb
Chronicle Books, 1997

Rumplestiltskin
illustrated by Dale Gottlieb
Children's Television Workshop, 1997

Edward Plants a Garden
written and illustrated by Dale Gottlieb
Envision Books, 1998

Tulip Builds a Birdhouse
written and illustrated by Dale Gottlieb
Envision Books, 1998

Ask Babalouie
written and illustrated by Dale Gottlieb and Jane Burns
Chronicle Books, 1999

Hushabye, Baby Blue
written by Kathi Appelt and illustrated by Dale Gottlieb
Harper Growing Tree, 2000

Wise Gal Tarot
written and illustrated by Dale Gottlieb and Jane Burns
Crown Books, 2000

Selected Collections

Roger Allers
Ron Balzdorf
Jerry Belson
Lloyd Costen
Brian Grazer
Martin Grey
Susan Grode
Jay Howell
Anne-Marie Johnson
Lily Kilvert
Harley Kozak
Chris Lemmon
Peter MacNichol
Craig McCaw
Judith McConnel
Jason Robards Jr.
Jason Robards Sr.
Anita Roddick
Richard Simmons
Danielle Steele
Washington State Arts Commission/Art in Public Places Program:
- Child Study and Treatment Center, Tacoma
- Whitney Elementary School, Tacoma
- Clark College, Vancouver
- Seattle University/School of Law
- Redmond Junior High School, Redmond
- Horace Mann Elementary School, Redmond
- Whitney Elementary School, Yakima

Gallery Representation

Virginia Breier Gallery, San Francisco
Lucia Douglas Gallery, Bellingham
Every Picture Tells A Story, Santa Monica, California
Gallery 500, Philadelphia
L'Attitude Gallery, Sarasota, Florida
Pismo Gallery, Denver
William Zimmer Gallery, Mendicino, California

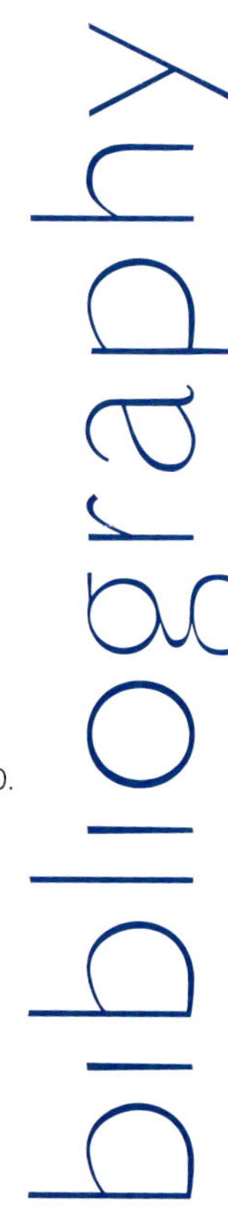

1992

Farr, Sheila. "Representational, Political, Symbolic Exhibits." *Bellingham Herald,* October 20.

1994

Bikman, Margaret. "Gallery Puts on the Dog." *Bellingham Herald,* September 8.

Hackett, Regina. "Art Notes." *Seattle Post Intelligencer,* September 14.

Rodger, Nelda. "Western Trade Winds." *Azure* (March/April): 22.

St. John Kelly, Erin. Book review of *Taxi! Taxi!* (children's book). *New York Times Book Review,* September 25.

Updike, Robin. "Fall Array." *Seattle Times,* September 8.

1995

Leimbach, Dulcie. "Rugs Woven from Stories." *New York Times,* May 18.

1996

Caba, Susan. "Design of the Week." *Philadelphia Inquirer,* July 19.

Enbysk, Liz. "Wool and Whimsy." *Tableaux* (June/July): 10.

Heffley, Lynne. "Magic Carpet Ride." *Los Angeles Times,* May 29.

"New Works." *Fiber Arts* (January/February): 19.

Raw Vision, no. 16 (fall): 22–23. (Exhibition listing with color plate.)

Seattle Weekly, December 18. (Exhibition listing with color plate.)

"Tread Softly." *Buzz* 7, no. 4 (May): 30.

1997

Daniels, Hope. "On the Cutting Edge." *American Style* (fall): 33.

Humphrey, Linda, and Paula Tully Gold. "All Eyes on Hue." *Better Homes and Gardens* (fall): 66–73.

1998

Dale Gottlieb: Story Rugs. Exh. cat. Seattle: Davidson Gallery. Text by Mia McEldowney.

Greco, JoAnn. "Upstairs, Downstairs." *Niche* (autumn): 38.

"Touched by Tibet." *Metropolitan Home* (July/August): 32.

Walker, Hollis. "Whimsy for Freedom." *Pasatiempo* (March).

1999

Bertelsen, Anne. "Art Underfoot." *Sunset Magazine* (February): 108.

2000

Basye, Alison. "Mixed Company." *Seattle Magazine* (October): 70.

Cohen, Fiona. "Exhibit Raises Profile of Children's Illustration." *Bellingham Herald,* March 2.

"Predict This!" *Working Mother* (December/January): 74.

2001

Goldberg, no. 14 (winter): 119. (Painting used in Jordi Savall's "Travel Notes.")

2002

Backer, Noelle. "Dale Gottlieb: Story Rugs." *Fiber Arts* 29, no. 3 (November/December): 30.

Relyea, Kie. "Art Under Fire." *Bellingham Herald,* February 27.

Works in the Exhibition

Rugs

Boy Angel, 1994 (p. 24)
Hand-knotted wool rug
4 × 4 ft.
Collection of Daria and Brad Smith

Sojourner Truth, 1994 (p. 31)
Hand-knotted wool rug
12 × 2½ ft.
Collection of the Bachhuber Family

Hallelujah, 1995 (p. 25)
Hand-knotted wool rug
4½ × 3½ ft.
Collection of Steve and Gina Chastain

My Eyes Have Seen the Glory, 1995 (p. 33)
Hand-knotted wool rug
9 × 6 ft.
Courtesy of the artist and Lucia Douglas Gallery

Sister Gertrude Morgan, 1995 (p. 28)
Hand-knotted wool rug
7 × 5 ft.
Collection of Clifford and Eileen Freed

Tread Softly, 1995 (p. 21)
Hand-knotted wool rug
10 × 8 ft.
Collection of Paul and Linda Niebanck

Tuskegee Airmen, 1995 (p. 29)
Hand-knotted wool rug
7 × 5 ft.
Courtesy of the artist and Lucia Douglas Gallery

Conversation, 1997 (p. 20)
Hand-knotted wool rug
7 × 5½ ft.
Collection of Troy Comfort

Hold, 1998 (p. 41)
Hand-knotted wool rug
7 × 5 ft.
Collection of Richard and Brenda Albert

Mr. Bill Traylor, 1998 (p. 32)
Hand-knotted wool rug
7 × 5 ft.
Collection of Richard and Brenda Albert

Shylock, 1998 (p. 43)
Hand-knotted wool rug
10 × 8 ft.
Courtesy of the artist and Lucia Douglas Gallery

Strange Fruit, 1998 (p. 35)
Hand-knotted wool rug
10 × 8 ft.
Courtesy of the artist and Lucia Douglas Gallery

Anne Frank, 2000 (pp. 12–13)
Hand-knotted wool rug
2½ × 12 ft.
Courtesy of the artist and Lucia Douglas Gallery

Pavel Friedman, 2000 (p. 22)
Hand-knotted wool rug
5 × 3½ ft.
Courtesy of the artist and Lucia Douglas Gallery

Terezin, 2000 (p. 19)
Hand-knotted wool rug
5 × 3½ ft.
Courtesy of the artist and Lucia Douglas Gallery

Gathering Strength, 2002 (p. 14)
Hand-knotted wool rug
5 × 3½ ft.
Courtesy of the artist and Lucia Douglas Gallery

Happier Times, 2002 (detail, p. 37)
Hand-knotted wool rug
9 × 6¾ ft.
Courtesy of the artist and Lucia Douglas Gallery

Happy Times, 2002 (p. 38)
Hand-knotted wool rug
9 × 6¾ ft.
Courtesy of the artist and Lucia Douglas Gallery

More Happy Times, 2002 (p. 39)
Hand-knotted wool rug
9 × 6¾ ft.
Courtesy of the artist and Lucia Douglas Gallery

His Holiness the Dalai Lama, 2003 (p. 40)
Hand-knotted wool rug
10 × 8 ft.
Courtesy of the artist and Lucia Douglas Gallery

Hope to Change, 2003 (pp. 26–27)
Hand-knotted wool rug
7 × 10 ft.
Courtesy of the artist and Lucia Douglas Gallery

King, 2003 (detail, p. 30; p. 31)
Hand-knotted wool rug
13 × 2½ ft.
Courtesy of the artist and Lucia Douglas Gallery

Paintings

Chicken, 1997 (p. 51)
Oil on paper
40 × 30 in.
Collection of the artist

Goodbye Miss Adlonia, 1997 (p. 47)
Oil on paper
60 × 40 in.
Collection of the artist

Gifted I, 1999 (p. 56)
Oil on paper
40 × 30 in.
Collection of Julie Shapiro

Blue Bohemian Stage, 2000 (p. 57)
Oil on paper
40 × 60 in.
Collection of Soraya Haeri

Free Moment, 2000 (p. 55)
Oil on canvas
40 × 60 in.
Collection of the artist

Friedle, 2000 (pp. 52–53)
Oil on paper
40 × 60 in.
Collection of Jackie Kallay

Gathering Strength, 2000 (p. 48)
Oil on paper
22 × 30 in.
Collection of Charles Fontaine

Survivor, 2000 (p. 54)
Oil on canvas
48 × 60 in.
Collection of the artist

Philadelphia, 2001 (p. 46 top)
Oil on paper
40 × 60 in.
Collection of the artist

Rilke, 2001 (p. 49)
Oil on paper
40 × 60 in.
Collection of Denise Black

I Am Too Alone in the World and Not Alone Enough, 2002 (p. 46 bottom)
Oil on paper
40 × 60 in.
Collection of the artist

Neesey, 2002 (p. 50)
Oil on canvas
48 × 36 in.
Collection of the artist

sponsors / staff

The essence of all beautiful art, all great art, is gratitude. —Friedrich Nietzsche

Catalogue Underwriters

Marquand Books, Inc.
Alan and Zelda Gottlieb
Troy Comfort
Susan A. Grode
Louis Van Doren and Barbara Congdon
La Fiamma Wood Fire Pizza

Catalogue Sponsors

Richard and Brenda Albert
Anna Aliotti
Barbara Murphy Interiors, Inc.
Denise Black
Jane Burns
Gina and Steve Chastain
Martin and Marilyn Colby
Sybil W. Conner
Carolyn Coughlin and Lars Crabo
Ronald and Anne Hathaway Crutcher
Jack Delay and Patricia Decker
The DiPaolo Foundation
Michael Fish
David and Amy Wergen Gould
Diane and Marc Grainer
Rita Greenfield
IMCO General Construction
Julie Lee and Walter Ingram
Eloise Marcella Iwersen
Kate Joyce Company
Barbara Lancaster
Thomas and Ellen M. Baratz Likovich
Lisa Ershig Interiors
Deborah Loober
Lucia Douglas Gallery
Martin and Didy Lutz
Ann Morris
Cameron Munro
Larry and Maria Elena O'Connell
Joni Papp
Helen Rachlin
Ruth Rachlin
Marcia Van Doren
Karin M. Webster
Tom Wood and Pam Brownell
Patricia Woodall

Exhibition Sponsors

The Starbucks Foundation
Starbucks Coffee Company
Peoples Bank
Southern Poverty Law Center
Creation Ground Media LLC
Lapchi Hand-Woven Decorative Carpets
Community Food Co-op

Whatcom Museum of History & Art

Administrative
Thomas A. Livesay, Director
Shirley Schroeder, Executive Administrative Assistant

Accounting
Judy Frost, Accounting Technician

Collections
Janis Olson, Curator of Collections
Nancy Deasy, Museum Assistant

Development
Kathleen Iwersen, Development Director
Tamara Tregoning, Membership Coordinator

Education
Richard Vanderway, Curator of Education and Public Programs
Mary Jo Maute, Education Assistant, Volunteer Interpreter Coordinator

Exhibits
Scott Wallin, Exhibits Chief
Lisa Van Doren, Curator of Art
Curt Mahle, Exhibitions and Facilities Assistant

Facilities
Patrick Dowling, Facilities Manager
Nancy Grinstead, Custodian
Glenda Albert, Security Information Attendant
Adam Jackman, Security Information Attendant
Katharine Jacobson, Security Information Attendant
Todd Warger, Security Information Attendant
Neil Weber, Security Information Attendant

Photo Archives
Toni Nagel, Photo Archivist, Curator of History
Jeff Jewell, Photo Historian, Archival Technician

Public Relations
Annette Bagley, Public Relations Consultant
Deanna Zipp, Secretary

Whatcom Children's Museum
Bev Wiltshire, Whatcom Children's Museum Operations Manager
Susie Burnett, Whatcom Children's Museum Education Coordinator
Marion Crew, Attendant
Trischa Farrer, Attendant
Aleda Rabel, Attendant
Seth Spangler, Attendant
Betsy Stalter, Attendant
Noah Wass, Attendant

artist's statement

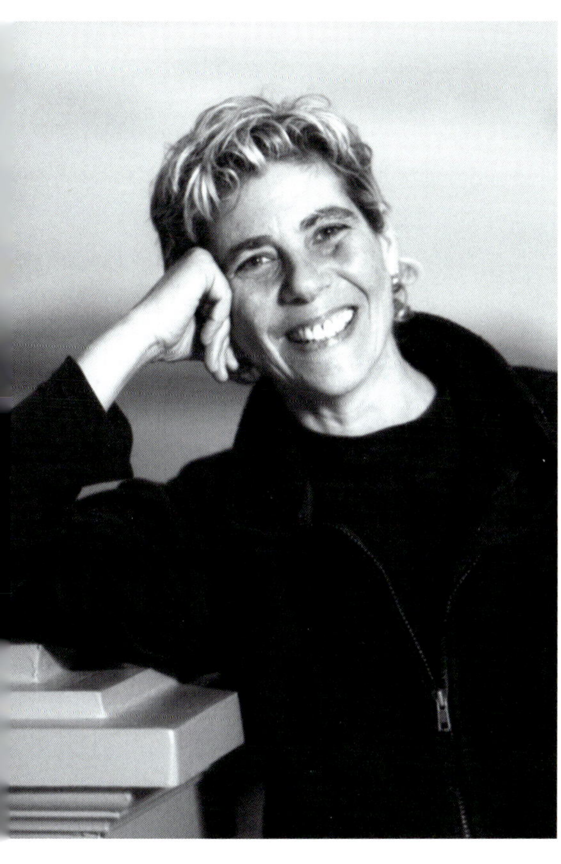

Perhaps the only true measure of *my gratitude to the Whatcom Museum of History & Art is the feel of my pulse when I think of the opportunity they have given me. My heartbeat soars to a dangerously high rate, which can only be calmed by prescriptives! My family, friends, and community have also supported this exhibition and accompanying catalogue, which I hope can serve as another small bridge to the other side of oppression and prejudice: freedom and awareness.*

The art and culture of other peoples move me to feel and understand more deeply the essential reasons for my own life, namely, to be of service through my work, to nurture others, to laugh and cry often, and to cause some trouble now and then.

It is such an exciting honor to bring peoples' stories—of their struggles for freedom—to a sometimes larger-than-life medium, a Tibetan rug. It's no accident that Lobsang Tenzing and I have become collaborators. We share a certain legacy of ancestral annihilation and both feel compelled to try to fight ignorance using our work as our medium and voice.

I have been blessed with the curse of an underdog's heritage. And, like Avis, we try harder to get to the same place. I hope to see you there.

Dale Gottlieb

Bellingham, Washington, 2003

With special thanks to Kathleen Iwersen, Tom Livesay, Mary Jo Maute, Lisa Van Doren, Scott Wallin, and Marquand Books. Hats off to Andrea Tiernan's third-grade class at Alderwood Elementary for their thoughtful work in art and storytelling. May their respect for diversity be contagious.

Whatcom Museum of History & Art
121 Prospect Street
Bellingham, WA 98225
www.whatcommuseum.org

This catalogue was published in conjunction with the exhibition *Story Rugs—Tales of Freedom: The Work of Dale Gottlieb*, November 16, 2003–March 7, 2004.

Library of Congress Control Number: 2003109406
ISBN: 0-938506-10-2

Distributed by
University of Washington Press
P.O. Box 50096
Seattle, WA 98145-5096
www.washington.edu/uwpress

Front cover: *Hope to Change*, 2003 (detail), pp. 26–27
Back cover: *Shylock*, 1998 (detail), p. 43
Endsheets: *Happier Times; Happy Times;* and *More Happy Times* (details; all part of the *Happy Series*, 2002), pp. 37, 38, and 39
Page 1: *Conversation*, 1997 (detail), p. 20
Page 2: *Hope to Change*, 2003, pp. 26–27
Page 3: *Boy Angel*, 1994 (top, detail), p. 24; childhood art by the artist (bottom)
Page 4: *Terezin*, 2000 (detail), p. 19
Page 5: childhood art by the artist
Page 6: *Hallelujah*, 1995 (detail), p. 25
Page 8: The artist and her brother Martin in Brooklyn, New York, late 1950s (top); childhood art by the artist (center and bottom)
Page 9: Lobsang Tenzing with his wife and children
Page 10: Hari Ram at work, graphing, weaving, and sewing a label on a rug
Page 44: *Rilke*, 2001 (detail), p. 49

Photography credits:
Eduardo Calderón: pp. 11, 14, 28
Roderick Del Pozo: pp. 4, 19, 22, 44, 47–57
Alan Gottlieb: p. 8 (top)
Spike Mafford: front cover, back cover, end sheets, pp. 2, 6, 10 (bottom), 12, 15, 16, 25–27, 30, 31 (left), 37–40, 46, 63
Alan Sanders: pp. 3 (bottom), 5, 8
Dan Sheehan: back cover insert
Lobsang Tenzing: pp. 9, 10 (top)
William Wickett: pp. 1, 3 (top), 20, 21, 24, 31 (right), 32, 33, 35, 41, 43

Edited by Michelle Piranio
Proofread by Sharon Vonasch
Designed by John Hubbard
Typeset by Jennifer Sugden
Color separations by iocolor, Seattle
Produced by Marquand Books, Inc., Seattle
www.marquand.com
Printed and bound by C&C Offset Printing Co., Ltd., China

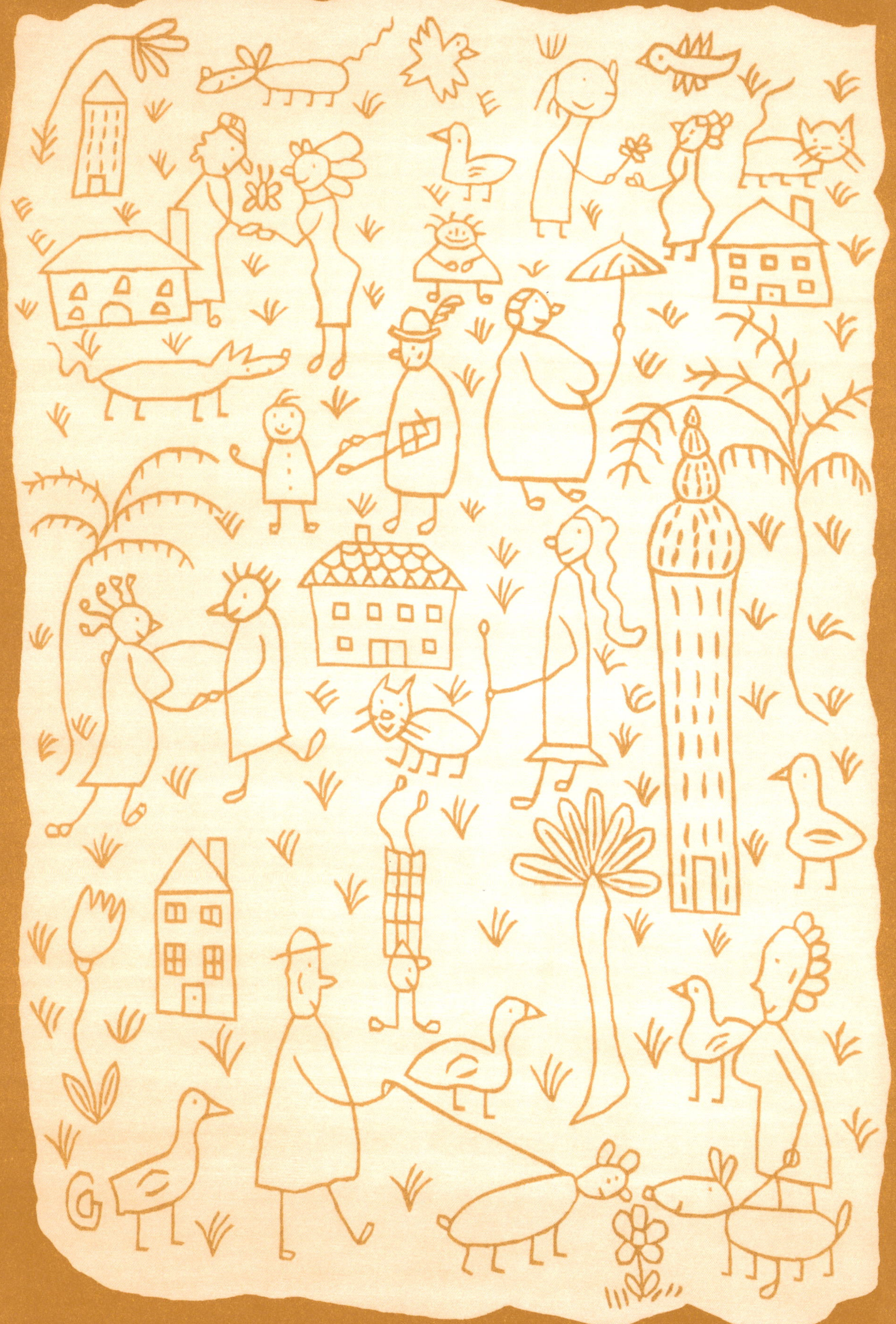

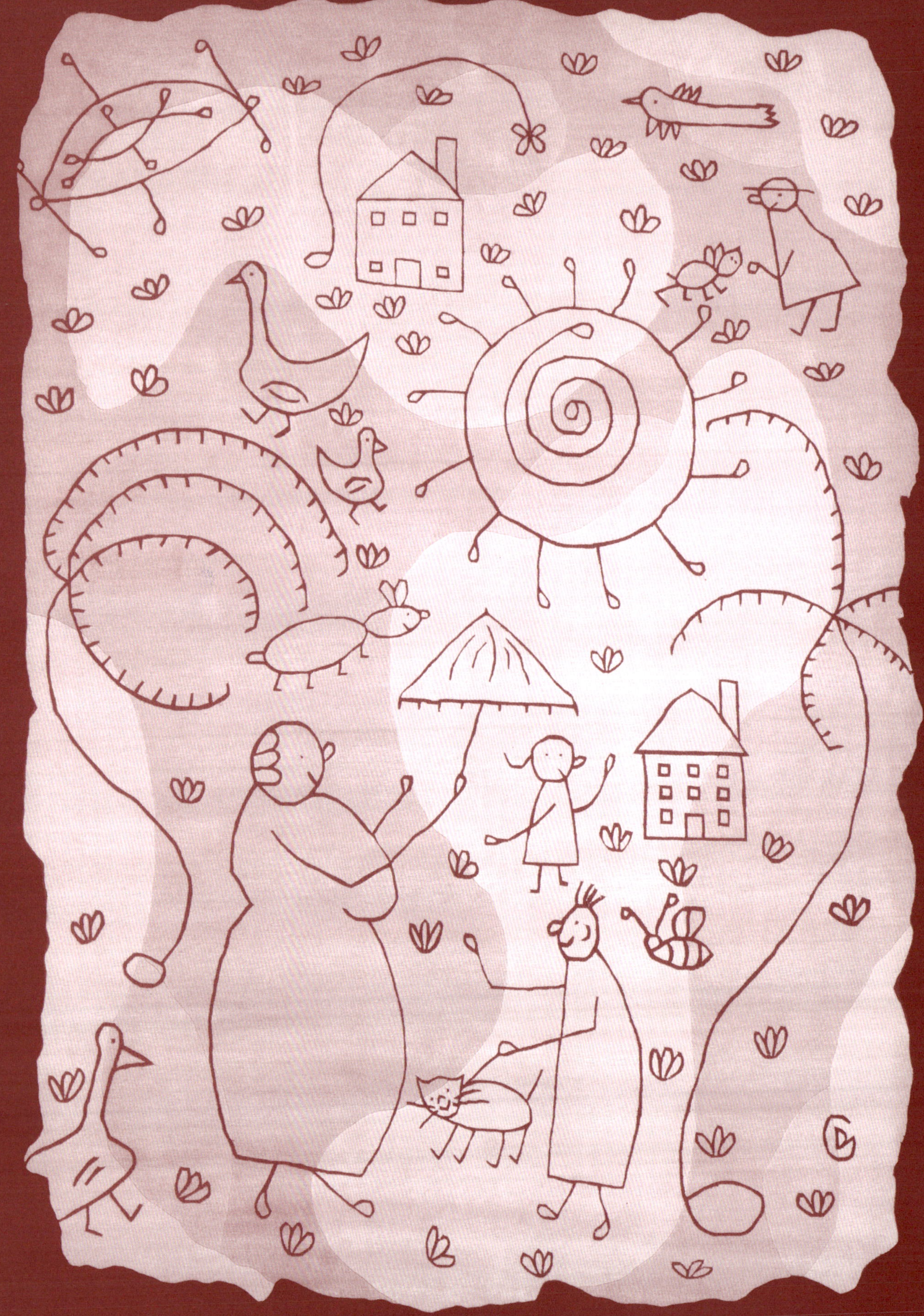